Why did Ancient States Collapse?

About Access Archaeology

Access Archaeology offers a different publishing model for specialist academic material that might traditionally prove commercially unviable, perhaps due to its sheer extent or volume of colour content, or simply due to its relatively niche field of interest. This could apply, for example, to a PhD dissertation or a catalogue of archaeological data.

All *Access Archaeology* publications are available as a free-to-download pdf eBook and in print format. The free pdf download model supports dissemination in areas of the world where budgets are more severely limited, and also allows individual academics from all over the world the opportunity to access the material privately, rather than relying solely on their university or public library. Print copies, nevertheless, remain available to individuals and institutions who need or prefer them.

The material is refereed and/or peer reviewed. Copy-editing takes place prior to submission of the work for publication and is the responsibility of the author. Academics who are able to supply print-ready material are not charged any fee to publish (including making the material available as a free-to-download pdf). In some instances the material is type-set in-house and in these cases a small charge is passed on for layout work.

Our principal effort goes into promoting the material, both the free-to-download pdf and print edition, where *Access Archaeology* books get the same level of attention as all of our publications which are marketed through e-alerts, print catalogues, displays at academic conferences, and are supported by professional distribution worldwide.

The free pdf download allows for greater dissemination of academic work than traditional print models could ever hope to support. It is common for a free-to-download pdf to be downloaded hundreds or sometimes thousands of times when it first appears on our website. Print sales of such specialist material would take years to match this figure, if indeed they ever would.

This model may well evolve over time, but its ambition will always remain to publish archaeological material that would prove commercially unviable in traditional publishing models, without passing the expense on to the academic (author or reader).

Why did Ancient States Collapse?

The dysfunctional state

Malcolm Levitt

Access Archaeology

Archaeopress Publishing Ltd
Summertown Pavilion
18-24 Middle Way
Summertown
Oxford OX2 7LG

www.archaeopress.com

ISBN 978-1-78969-302-7
ISBN 978-1-78969-303-4 (e-Pdf)

© M Levitt and Archaeopress 2019

The cover image is from a photograph taken by the author at the Maya site of Quirigua, Guatemala.

This work is licensed under a Creative Commons Attribution-NonCommercial-NoDerivatives 4.0 International (CC BY-NC-ND 4.0)

This book is available direct from Archaeopress or from our website www.archaeopress.com

Contents

Abstract iii
Preface v
Acknowledgments vii

I. Introduction: meaning, origins, fragility, cyclicality and collapse of ancient states 1
    Meaning 1
    Increasing complexity 1
    Farming 2
    Population growth 2
    Chiefdoms and pathways to states 2
    Competition, coercion, consensus 3
    Fragility 3
    Cyclicality 3
    Meaning of collapse 4
    Evidence of collapse 6
    Explanations of collapse 7

II. The dysfunctional state 9
    The state's core functions 9
    Conditions necessary for fulfilling the state's functions 9
    Collapse as dysfunction 10

III. Egyptian Old Kingdom 11
    Collapse 11
    Explanations of collapse 12

IV. Mycenaean Palace States 15
    Collapse 16
    Explanations of collapse: Earthquakes 16
    Climate change 17
    Decline in foreign trade 17
    Warfare techniques 18
    Sea Peoples 18
    Interstate Mycenaean warfare 18
    Internal strife 18
    Rural collapse 19
    Systems collapse 19
    Conclusions 19

V. The Western Roman Empire 21
What Collapsed? 22
What caused collapse? 23
Christianity 23
Barbarians 23
Failure of the Eastern Empire to help 24
Internal strife 24
Economic factors 25
Natural Disasters 25
Conclusions 26

VI. Classic Mayan collapse 27
Collapse 27
Causes of collapse 28
Climate Change, Drought 28
Internal and external strife and violence 29

VII. Inequality 31
Inequality and state collapse 31
Inequality and violence in ancient states 31
Evidence of popular resentment 32
Conclusions 33

VIII. Summary and Conclusions 35

Bibliography 37

Abstract

Ancient states were rooted in agriculture, sedentism and population growth. They were fragile and prone to collapse, but there is no consensus on the causes or meaning of collapse, and there is an ongoing debate about the importance, nature and even existence of state-wide collapse

Explanations of collapse in terms of competing mono-causal factors are found inferior to those incorporating dynamic, interactive systems. It is proposed that collapse should be explained as failure to fulfil the ancient state's core functions: assurance of food supplies, defence against external attack, maintenance of internal peace, imposition of its will throughout its territory, enforcement of state-wide laws, and promotion of an ideology to legitimise the political and social status quo.

To fulfil these functions certain necessary conditions must be met. The legitimacy of the political and social status quo, including the distribution of political power and wealth, needs to be accepted; the state should be able to extract sufficient resources to fulfil its functions such as defence; it must be able to enforce its decisions; the ruling elite should share a common purpose and actions; the society needs to reflect a shared spirit (*asibaya*) and purpose across elites and commoners who believe it is worthy of defence.

Weaknesses and failure to meet any condition can interact to exacerbate the situation: maladministration, corruption and elite preoccupation with self aggrandisement can induce fiscal weakness, reduced military budgets and further invasion; it can induce neglect of key infrastructures (especially water management). Inequality, a commonly neglected factor despite ancient texts, can erode asibaya and legitimacy and alienate commoners from defence of the state.

These themes are explored in relation to the Egyptian Old Kingdom, Mycenae, the Western Roman Empire (WRE), and the Maya. They all exhibit, to varying degrees, weaknesses in meeting the above conditions necessary for stability. (Some of the explanatory political and social factors involved have modern analogies but that issue is not examined).

Preface

This publication is an extended version of my MA dissertation for the University College London Institute of Archaeology. In particular, this text proposes an explanation of ancient state collapse in terms of dysfunctionality. It has its origins in my interest, while a Hallsworth Fellow in economics at Manchester University, in reasons for revolution, civil war and state collapse in modern states receiving aid from Western sources. This work was aborted when I joined HM Treasury.

As an academic and as an official I have long had an interest in inequality and found that no studies have been made of the role of inequality in the collapse of ancient states despite assertions by Aristotle and De Tocqueville about this. Some recent studies have commented on the impact of collapse on inequality but not the converse and a recent study of ancient inequality barely mentions the subject. I made less progress than I had intended because of paucity of data which reflects neglect by archaeologists, the subject of my July 2019 article in Cliodynamics.

Acknowledgments

Professor Stephen Shennan provided regular advice, encouragement and helpful criticism throughout the preparation of my dissertation. Professor Todd Whitelaw volunteered unstinting guidance to helpful studies of Mycenae. Dr. Claudia Naeser advised me on essential material on the Egyptian Old Kingdom. Dr Benet Salway pointed me to studies of Roman peasant revolts. Dan Hoyer suggested valuable improvements to my critical treatment of the literature on collapse. Charlotte Butterworth and Cherith Hateley assisted with the graphics. Maisie Levitt typed the bibliography from my nearly illegible manuscript.

Any errors and other flaws are entirely my responsibility.

I. Introduction: meaning, origins, fragility, cyclicality and collapse of ancient states

The focus of this text is on the nature and possible explanations of the collapse of ancient states. The evidence and possible explanations for collapse are investigated with respect to four case studies. It is argued below that collapse should be studied as the dynamic interactions between explanatory factors sometimes regarded in the literature as rival explanations within a conceptual framework that emphasises dysfunctionality.

Some of the explanatory factors have parallels in current western societies, however this theme is not explored (but see Turchin 2016, Ortmans, Mazzeo and Mescherina 2017).

Meaning

The meaning of the terms 'state 'and 'civilisation' need to be explained before the question of what collapsed can be considered. In principle states are usually recognised as institutionalised, centralised government structures with hierarchical administrations ideally staffed by officials appointed because of competence rather than kinship with the rulers (Cherry 1978, Yoffee2005). States have authority to impose decisions by coercion and to take resources from the public including products, money or labour (corvee). This portrayal has been dismissed as a mere check list (Legarra Herrero 2016) but it is a useful device that helps to differentiate states and civilisations.

Civilisations have been defined as *'the social order and set of shared values in which states are culturally embedded'* (Yoffee 2005 p. 17). Different states can share a common civilisation, such as the Mycenaean and Mayan city states; and states can collapse but the civilisation continues, like the Mesopotamian states (Yoffee and Cowgill 1988 p 18).

Given the difficulty of distinguishing between states and non states such as chiefdoms in the archaeological record Tainter (1988) prefers to use the term 'complex society' and to comment on more or less complex societies; Fried (1960 p 728) defined complexity as 'organisation of society on a non-kinship basis' (cited by Yoffee 2005 p 16).

The term 'complex society' has been criticised by McGuire (1983 p 92) as imprecise, embracing too heterogeneous a range of variables that describe complexity that are not necessarily correlated. Nonetheless 'Complexity' is an accommodating and flexible concept, otherwise endless disputes would ensue over just how many attributes need to exist before one can say whether a state is present or not? (Renfrew (1972 P 369) questioned whether Mycenaean polities were truly states or chiefdoms).

Increasing complexity

Over the past ten millennia societies have become more complex; small communities have coalesced (whether consensually or coercively). Domestication of crops and livestock was gradually established, sedentism, ritual, economic specialisation, leadership, hierarchies including elites, institutionalisation of social interaction and direction, and taxation emerged, as did amounting to increasing complexity and state formation. Inequality increased; it was not new and had existed in Palaeolithic hunter-gatherer societies, indicated by lavish or ornate grave goods such as those found at Sunghir (Trinkhaus et. al., 2015) or Dolni Vestonice (Cook, 2013) but such occasional examples cannot reveal the extent of hunter-gatherer inequality.

Farming

No state emerged without the presence of farming (Yoffee 2005). Although farming was necessary for state formation it was not sufficient: crop management and animal husbandry appeared in Mesopotamia long before the appearance of states. Farming enabled but alone it did not cause state formation and farming did not need states (Scott 2017, pp. 22-24).

The key dimension of farming needed for state formation and sustenance was grain: it was a sound base for taxation. Moreover it could be stored and used to pay labourers and soldiers (Scott 2017 pp116-119). It provided ruling elites with a foundation for expropriation and hence economic and political control and was a crucial ingredient in farming's contribution to state formation.

Population growth

Although states eventually evolved following sedentism and agrarianism (Cherry 1984 pp 29-32) neither was sufficient for state formation. Yoffee argues that the catalyst was population growth, which Shennan (2018 p.7) shows was facilitated by farming because it improved diets, female energy and fertility, thereby enabling more children to be borne and to survive as mothers had more time for child care. It required administrative machinery for managing, storing and distributing agricultural surpluses, tasks beyond the capacity of pre-state entities including chiefdoms. They relied on kinsfolk not professional managers. (Conceivably they could have subdivided but this would have been resisted by chiefs and could be difficult to identify archaeologically.) The assurance of food supplies and distribution can be regarded as the *founding function* of the ancient state if this hypothesis is accepted. From this perspective the state was necessary to assure food supplies when population growth surged. A different but complementary view is that of Scott (Scott 2017 p. 129) who suggested that food in the form of grain was necessary for the maintenance of the state once it was established: it is measurable, storable, available for remunerating workers and soldiers and, above all, taxable. So the assurance of food supplies being both a core function of the state and essential to its resource base it follows that failure of food supplies threatens state collapse.

Chiefdoms and pathways to states

Clearly something preceded them but by which processes did state emerge? Service (1962) proposed a unilineal trajectory running through bands, tribes and chieftains then states. Such a model does not allow for collapse and it has been described as merely taxonomic (Yoffee 2005 p. 32.

Yoffee (2005 pp. 34-36) suggests that the key to state formation was power based on three mutually reinforcing elements: economic power, meaning control of resources and material wealth; social power, including leadership of groups in what were horizontally segmented societies, whether because of ethnicity, family or locality; and military power, the control of armed supporters.

Economic power accumulated in Neolithic times when the more ambitious, energetic or luckier agriculturalists (with better land) supported the less fortunate when the latter suffered poor harvests, and so became indebted to the better off who, over time, accumulated wealth, status and power, especially as rights of ownership and inheritance became accepted (Bogerhoff, 2010; Shennan, 2011).

Leaders of communities emerged through mutually reinforcing growing wealth and power which induced competition between such people. Competition between the leaders of rival communities led to the dominance of some communities over others and statehood, as in the case of competition between Upper and Lower Egypt that lead to unification under rule from Memphis (Middleton 2017 p. 86).

Competition, coercion, consensus

Competition and the development of hierarchies of client-patron relationships were reconciled under centralised leadership in states (Yoffee 2005 p.42). But competition and hierarchy sit alongside human capacity for cooperation and sharing (Feinman 2011 pp. 21-26). From this two possible state formations or structures emerge.

The consensual model is expressed by Ibn Khaldun's concept of *'asabiya'* (1337), a sense of group empathy and especially present in desert tribes such as Berbers, which gave rise to communal, urban living under benign leaders. But over time elites developed and became self-centred, asabiya eroded, leading to collapse. Turchin (2003 p. 32) asked why people should give up freedom to participate in states in the first place and argues it is in the expectation of mutual benefit. He refers to the concept of a 'social contract' which implies that in surrendering a degree of personal freedom to a state, people expect to benefit from greater security, peace and prosperity; conflict and liberty are reconciled in an integrated structure which falls apart when states fail to deliver what was expected. .

The consensus model implies stability without coercion and a relatively egalitarian distribution of income and wealth. The conflict or competitive model implies coercion, low popular participation in politics and greater inequality. However the consensual, egalitarian model has probably been less common and shorter lived, examples being relatively few, such as the redistributive efforts of the Gracci brothers in Rome in the 2nd century BCE. Nonetheless Legarra Herrero (2014) argues that archaeological evidence demonstrates the communal nature of Minoan palatial states.

This implies constraints on freedom to escape the 'social cage', which was not an issue for hunter gatherers (Mann 1986 pp. 39-41. The reconciliation of individual aims with order and state rule is the role of legitimacy: the acceptance by society of the right of rulers to govern and of existing inequality. Threats to legitimacy risk collapse. In ancient states legitimacy was buttressed by the divinity of rulers, ritual, feasting, exotic symbols and regalia, and the loyalty of the military and the elite support group, as with the Egyptian Old kingdom and the Maya. But ultimately it depended on the ability of the state to deliver what was expected: stable supplies of sustenance, internal law and order, defence against external attack

Fragility

Ancient states were fragile, being exposed to internal threats, including intra-elite and centre-province tensions, external threats such as invasion, human- induced ecological degradation, natural disasters, and the risk of infectious disease induced by the agrarian revolution Scott (2017, passim, citing Groube 1996). This risk is associated with sedentism, the growth of population density and proximity to domesticated animals. Cook (2013, pp. 5-6) argues that diphtheria, influenza, mumps, whooping cough and tuberculosis are similar pathogens to those present in Eurasian domesticated animals and *'probably or possibly reached humans from domesticates'* (Wolfe et. al. 2007 p. 218). The sustainability of these diseases *'rose with population density'* (Dobson and Cooper 1969). Thus, on the above evidence, ironically, the Neolithic both bred the roots of state formation (sedentism) and a significant contribution to state fragility: infectious disease. However Gagneux (2012) reports genetic studies indicating that 'modern' TB originated in Africa, from which it spread 70,000 ago: long before the Neolithic. But human animal-transmission is not disputed, if animals but not humans are initially infected at a location, nor is the risk of contagion in densely populated areas contradicted.

Cyclicality

State formation and collapse are sometimes viewed as cycles of birth, stability and collapse. Such a cyclical view contradicts evolutionist unlinearity.

The earliest cyclical model was that of Ibn Khaldun: the culture of *asabiya* which underpinned state stability weakened over time as population grew, ruling dynasties and elites lost their feeling of duty towards the population, alienation between ruler and ruled grew, social fragmentation and collapse followed, desert tribes with their asabiya moved in and the cycle recommenced.

Joyce Marcus' 'Dynamic Model' (Marcus 1998) notes a cycle of state formation, expansion incorporating smaller polities, followed by fragmentation into smaller states among Mayan and Mesopotamian states. Collapse is part of a normal pattern of behaviour, not an unnatural or anachronistic event. But such a description of events is not an explanation of why formation and collapse occur. Demarest (1997) claims that Marcus' supposed Mayan cycle was no such thing: Mayan states followed a *'unidirectional series of steps towards fragmentation'* (Demarest, cited by Middleton p.38).

The seminal cyclical approach to instability and collapse is that of Peter Turchin. His 'clyiodynamics' model of growth and collapse formalised and quantified cycles of state formation and collapse (Turchin 2003, *Historical Dynamics*). The most advanced analysis of this kind is in *Secular Cycles* by Turchin and Nefedov, 2009, covering four case studies. Some 25 processes are included such as elite dynamics, state strength, communal solidarity, tax revenue and public spending. Turchin and Nefedov reviewed the data for eight cycles in four countries and concluded their model was confirmed. Citing Goldstone (1991), they see population growth as the trigger for political collapse: population growth raises the demand for food but diminishing marginal returns mean output fails to match rising demand.

When population density rises towards the carrying capacity of the available natural resources land, rents and food prices rise, real wages fall, peasants quit the land for urban areas, elites prosper from rents and land price increase, inequality grows, food reserves are depleted, mortality increase, famines can arise, and food riots occur. As long as the rulers maintain support of the military and are united popular uprisings fail – unless they attract leadership and organisation from disaffected members of the elite or army.

But slowing economic growth ensures declining tax revenues; privileges and elite ranks are sold to raise state funds but the expansion of the elite means falling elite wealth per capita, inducing rising resentment among members of the elite which in turn exacerbates oppression of the peasantry towards starvation, and intra-elite competition. The ability of the state to maintain internal stability is damaged; then fiscal bankruptcy and loss of military control induce violent elite and popular uprisings; civil war and the collapse of central authority. Overall the theoretical model is convincing although some of the evidence is contentious.

A different cyclical account of collapse and renewal is that of resilience theorists such as Redman (2005) who hypothesises an adaptive cycle embracing *exploitation* of a colonised area then *conservation* when energy and material are accumulated and stored, followed by *release* involving increasing fragility with degradation of the landscape and possibly socio-ecological collapse then *reorganisation* into a new, innovative system. In such a model collapse is not an aberration but is normal. It stresses the human-ecological interface rather than socio-political complexity. A number of case studies illustrate the model. Redman (p.73) asserts collapse can arrive suddenly, in the accumulation or reorganisation phases in response to an external shock, so it is not a wholly endogenous explanation of collapse. Incorporating reorganisation, it emphasises the possibility of resilience (the capacity to absorb shocks and to reform) but *'it may offer nothing new in terms of explaining how collapse comes about'* (Middleton 2017 p. 46).

Meaning of collapse

The word 'collapse' implies the complete breakdown or failure of the entity in question, such as a state, with its political and administrative structures. But complications arise from this view of state collapse.

The first is that collapse is rarely distinguished from decline in the literature. Collapse implies finality, perhaps an event or at least something relatively rapid whereas decline suggests a drawn out process. However, as discussed below, some authorities claim collapse can be spread over a lengthy period, others stress rapidity and some assign no time scale at all. Some say any distinction is arbitrary. Although decline is often thought to lead to collapse, most famously Gibbon's *The Decline and Fall of the Roman Empire,* Bronson (1988) asserts, reasonably, that collapse is not the inevitable consequence of decline.

Secondly, collapse is regarded as rare if, as Eisenstadt commented (1998 p. 132), it is interpreted as *'the complete end of those political systems and their civilizational framework'.* Some degree of continuity is often present (Cowgill and Yoffee 1998) p. 132.

McAnany and Yoffee (2010) are sceptical about the very existence of collapse, stressing resilience and continuity. They warn (p. 6) that the presence of ruins or abandonment need not signal collapse but that the population adapted to new circumstance and moved on, although they are different perspectives of the same phenomenon. This should not be taken to mean that we should always dismiss ruins as evidence of collapse but one needs to be cautious if the presence of a ruin is not accompanied by other evidence. They emphasise society's resilience: the ability to absorb shocks and meet new challenges: *'on close inspection of archaeological records and documentary records or both, it becomes clear that human resilience is the rule rather than the exception' (p.10).* In support of this conclusion their book cites several case studies (but none of those discussed pp. 16-38 below) and challenges the assessment of collapse asserted by Diamond (1997, 2005). McAnany and Yoffee seem to define collapse as the elimination of all political, social, economic, ideological traditions and the previous material culture: this strict comprehensive picture of collapse is rarely found, some traditional cultural features continue, and this enables denial of collapse. None of this contradicts the possibility of collapse, which they see as part of an adaptive cycle, but that their position reinforces the need to be clear about what collapsed: political entities or civilisations. States may collapse politically, as in Mesopotamia or the Mayan and Mycenaean states, while elements of their civilisation lived on.

The first comprehensive treatment of the features of collapse is by Renfrew (1979.

Renfrew set out the main features of the collapse of centrally administered early states, including *'disappearance or reduction in the number of levels of hierarchy...fragmentation or disappearance of military organizations...eclipse of temples...loss of literacy... abandonment of public building...cessation of rich burials... collapse of centralized economy [including] market exchange coinage...reduced external trade...cessation of craft-specialist manufacture [and of] specialized or organized agricultural production...abandonment of settlements... flight to the hills...marked reduction in population density...'* (Renfew 1979, pp. 482-484). Later writers tended to go over the same ground, often without acknowledging Renfrew's original contribution, except for Tainter (1988).

For Tainter *'collapse is a political process... a society has collapsed when it displays a rapid, significant loss of an established level of social complexity'* (Tainter 1988 p.4). His focus is ostensibly on societies not states but it is difficult to disentangle them. His emphasis on the political process and rapidity separates him from several other contributors to the debate on collapse, although he accepts that collapse might take a few decades. He examined twenty states, civilisations or societies (the distinction does not seem significant for him), nine in greater detail, and identified eight processes and concluded that collapse involved at least some (how many is not discussed and he would probably say any numerical boundary would be arbitrary and unnecessary) including: less stratification and social differentiation; reduced economic specialisation; lower centralisation; reduced investment in the symbols of civilisation (monuments, art, literature); reduced information flows; a smaller state territory (Tainter 1988 pp.4-5).

Cowgill's and Yoffee's work on collapse (1988) covered five case studies by different authors. Their introduction expresses great scepticism about the very existence of collapse. because they emphasise the continuity of civilisations and do not appear to acknowledge instances of state political collapse although they were concerned to stress the difference between states and civilisations. They pray in aid (Cowgill and Yoffee p. 5) a claim that Tainter, the pioneer of cross country collapse analysis, found *'there wasn't any'* but Tainter (2006) says no such thing.

For Diamond (1997) the key feature of collapse is a major fall in population and or reduced political, economic and social complexity over an extended period of time and over a considerable area. This is in contrast with Tainter's emphasis on collapse as a rapid political process. While mentioning other factors his stress is on human-induced ecological disaster resulting from deliberate but short sighted choices. He cites several examples, all challenged by McAnany and Yoffee's book (2005 op. cit.), while admitting there is no *'case where a society's collapse can be attributed solely to environmental damage'* (Diamond 2005 p.182). Quirko (2005) argues convincingly that Diamond's case studies are about societies *'at the mercy of processes of which they have no awareness and cannot control, rather than choice'*.

Butzer and Endfield (2012, p.3628) reviewed twelve example of severe socio-political stress, of which seven suffered serious damage and five had the resilience to survive. They are sceptical of attempting cross-country correlations because individual chronologies are subject to large margins of error. They see collapse as featuring large scale social or spatial transformations with enduring impacts on *'environmental change and resilience...demography...socioeconomic patters...political or social structure and ideology...'*

Clearly there is no consensus on the definition of 'collapse', the time scale for collapse or whether what is collapsing is a state, a society or a civilisation.

The above shortcomings of generalisations about collapse induce Cumming and Peterson (2017) plea (p. 699) for a scientific, unambiguous and quantifiable approach to collapse. They do not provide a quantifiable model, they ignore the distinction between collapse of states and civilisations and their review of explanations offered for several collapses leaves key issues under-explored.

Evidence of collapse

Taking account of the literature summarised above and before proceeding to discussing four case studies of collapse a framework for considering evidence of their collapse is needed. Such evidence should contain at least some of the following features:

1. *the disappearance of or reduced central authority*
2. *fragmentation of a unified state*
3. *reduced territory*
4. *reduced social differentiation*
5. *increased number of violent deaths*
6. *abandonment and/or destruction of palaces, large houses*
7. *abandonment and/or destruction of settlements*
8. *ending of or reduced investment in large public buildings and funerary complexes*
9. *population fall and/or dispersal*
10. *economic decline, including agriculture, trade, craft production.*
11. *decline or ending of art, writing ,luxury good use and burial deposition*

To which should be added: evidence of *skeletal trauma*, indicating increased violence, especially if it can be correlated with evidence of contemporaneous civil disorder or invasion; or with increased inequality.

Explanations of collapse

Various potential explanations of collapse emerge from the literature cited above that need to be tested against the evidence from the four case studies examined below.

The potential explanations proposed can be summarised as:

1. *internal strife*: destabilising competition for power between ambitious elites and rulers or between competing elites; tension between the centre and the provinces; violent clashes between social classes and/or ethnicities.
2. *Loss of resilience* when the socio-political system is too inflexible to respond to new challenges.
3. *War with neighbours or invasion* : a violent challenge to stability, either directly or because it fatally exposes the cracks in society; barbarian invasion as a cause has been criticised by Bronson (1988, p. 201) who argues that barbarians, while often present at state collapse did not necessarily cause it
4. *excessive and/or regressive budget burdens*: excessive taxation can produce popular alienation especially if it is perceived to be the result of royal self indulgence, whether conspicuous consumption, lavish monumental construction or failed military adventures; regressive taxation alienates the poorer – those upon whom military recruitment depends
5. *natural disasters- earthquake or volcanic eruptions or climate change especially drought* are often proposed as causes of collapse, whether directly as when famine and popular attacks on palatial grain stores result, or indirectly when royal legitimacy is perceived to have been destroyed through withdrawal of the blessing of the gods; however chronologies of climate change are fraught with error (Dincauze 2000) and chronologies of climatic change and collapse can be difficult to correlate; and evidence of climate change and drought can be contentious
6. *human ecological damage* including soil degradation (because of excessively intensive exploitation) and deforestation, causing declining agricultural productivity and inability to meet foods needs
7. *inadequate resources to meet challenges*, meaning the exhaustion of treasuries and inability to fund and recruit military manpower, weakening state's defences
8. Tainter suggested an economic explanation: *when the marginal cost of complexity exceeds its marginal benefit collapse ensues*, although his evidence is contentious (Blanton 1990, Bowerstock 1991).
9. *systems collapse; adaptive systems, developed to cope with certain circumstances, become inflexible and cannot meet new challenges; positive feedbacks between destabilising factors induce a catastrophic chain reaction (Renfrew 1979)*
10. Complexity-induced collapse: '*...complex socio-political systems exhibit an internal dynamic which leads them to increased complexity [and the] more complex a system is the more liable it is to collapse*' (Dark, 1993, cited Cline 2014 p. 168.
11. *Cyclical normality*: cyclical models discussed earlier (pp. 7-9) regard collapse as a 'normal' feature of social behaviour but cyclicality as a concept is insufficient to explain particular collapses by itself.

A flaw in the collapse literature, except Butzer and Endfield 2012, is that it largely only incorporates collapsed states. Collapse study should incorporate samples of (i) states that did not collapse (e.g. other states or periods of stability in states that later or previously collapsed) but where factors suggested to explain collapse were present and (ii) collapsed states where some such factors were absent. In this way the probability of collapse associated with each 'explanatory factor' could be explored.

Other problems arise with explanations outlined above. They tend to be seen as competing alternatives whereas they are not mutually exclusive in reality. Another is oversimplification in implying a deterministic link between some alleged exogenous causal factor and its consequences, such as between drought and famine; clearly adverse rainfall, and temperature and their duration are truly exogenous but their impact also depends on precautionary measures such as flood control, irrigation and grain storage in areas prone to climatic volatility, such as those studied below.

A further weakness is that the possibility of *simultaneity* tends to be ignored: where a factor is both determined by another and determines the latter. Invasion might be induced because of perceived military weakness in the invaded state but military weakness may be caused by fiscal inadequacy due to loss of the agricultural tax base to invaders.

Three possible models of collapse emerge: mono-causal linear as when internal strife or invasion or drought-induced famines are of such a scale as to cause unavoidable collapse; the second combines linearity with both exogenous and endogenous factors present as when the effect of drought might have been mitigated by sufficient precautions (water management, grain storage) which were neglected because of internal strife; the third is a recursive dynamic systems model: invasion induced by internal strife and weakness, leading to erosion of the tax base and inability to resist further invasion.

Table 1 below illustrates some of the possibilities.

Conceivably internal strife, invasion or famine each alone might be sufficient to cause collapse but evidence from historical collapses suggest they are likely to be factors in a dynamic interactive process. The dynamic processes outlined above need to be set in a broader framework which is outlined below.

Table 1. Interactions between collapse and its explanatory factors

Variable to be explained	Explanatory variables
Collapse	Internal strife, invasion, famine
Internal strife	Dynastic and/or intra-elite violence
Invasion	Military capacity
Military capacity	Military budget
Military budget	State fiscal health
State fiscal health	Economic management
Economic management	Degree of internal strife
Famine	Climatic events, precautions
Precautions	Economic management

II. The dysfunctional state

The dynamic processes described above need to be set in a broader framework. States collapse when they can no longer perform their core functions but in order to fulfil those functions certain conditions need to be met.

The state's core functions

There is much debate on the functions of the modern state, especially its role relative to that of the private sector and with regard to macroeconomic stability. These issues can be bypassed here. The founding function of a stable ancient state was assurance of food supplies, the availability of which also provided the resources needed for the functioning of the state when appropriated. This was not only a matter in the hands of exogenous factors such as climate and weather but could also encompass the construction and maintenance of water management infrastructures, such as irrigation and flood control, and grain storage in the provision of which the state had agency.

Defence against external attack is a key function of any stable state and requires an army, whether a standing professional army as in the case of Rome or one raised in times of need (as was the case of the Egyptian Old Kingdom: Darnell J. and Menassa C. *Tutankhamen's Armies* 2007, Garcia J. *War in the Old Kingdom*), weaponry and fortifications: all costly and requiring appropriation of resources.

The maintenance of internal peace (law and order) and a legal system for regulating relations between citizens and between citizens and the state together with the means for enforcing state decisions and rules throughout its territory were recognised as important functions of ancient states (Roman law is well known but see also Mark J. 2017 *Ancient Egyptian* Law; for the comprehensive Maya legal system see Jamail Center for Legal Research, Tarlton Law Library, University of Texas).

Fundamental to the continuity of the ancient state was the promotion and maintenance of an ideology which legitimised the political and social status quo. This included the right of the ruling to rule and the distribution of wealth irrespective of the degree of inequality involved.

Other functions might be added from time to time, such as poor relief in the Roman republic and Empire but, arguably, this was not a core function crucial to the continuity of the state.

Conditions necessary for fulfilling the state's functions

Failure to fulfil its core functions threatened collapse but in order to execute those functions certain conditions had to be met. Probably the most important was acceptance of the legitimacy of the political and social status quo. This embraced not only acceptance by the commoners but also acceptance by the elites of the legitimacy of the ruling dynasty, especially its head, the supreme ruler. Without commoner acceptance uprisings and failure to support the state when under attack threatened the state's stability. Even coercive regimes need legitimacy: Pharonic legitimacy rested on the supposed divine status of the pharaohs, who, because of their closeness to the deities were able to guarantee rainfall and flood waters, the failure of which damaged the legitimacy of the king.

Elite disaffection meant failure to meet another condition for the continuity of a stable functioning state: cohesion of vision, purpose and action among the ruling elite. Without such cohesion internal challenges to the regime, possibly violent, would have threatened instability, fragmentation or collapse.

Additionally, effective action when the state came under exogenous threat, whether from external attack or natural disaster would have been difficult or impossible.

Cohesion among the elite needed to accompany cohesion across society as a whole: *asibaya*, the spirit of common purpose or the glue that held society together. It is essential to willingness to defend the state when under attack and to pay taxes. Erosion of asibaya when elites behave selfishly and inequality becomes extreme erodes the legitimacy of the status quo and threatens uprisings or even desertion to invaders (as in the case of barbarian attacks on Rome, see below).

In order to fulfil its core functions such as military defence or maintenance of key infrastructures as well as the maintenance of palatial structures, staff and ceremonies, the state needed to be able to extract sufficient resources, whether in kind, labour (corvee) or monetary taxation. Ineffective tax administration, corruption, diversion of revenues intended for the central treasury (as was done by provincial governors in the Egyptian Old Kingdom), resistance to higher tax burdens (as arose in the years of Diocletian's significant increases in taxation in Rome), erosion of the tax base through loss of territory to invaders (such as barbarian invasions of the Roman empire),granting of generous tax breaks to the elite, all weakened the state's capacity to fulfil its functions. A different threat to the state's resources is over-exploitation of the rural tax base, a case of killing the goose that lay the golden eggs, a possible factor in Mycenaean collapse (Cunliffe, 2008 p. 238; Maran, 2009 passim).

Collapse as dysfunction

Given the preceding arguments collapse can be regarded as the consequence of a dysfunctional state. But that is not sufficient to explain collapse: interactions among weaknesses and failures to meet the conditions need for a stable functioning state need to be recognised.

Diagram A illustrates the issues.

The remaining chapters discuss four case studies: the collapse of the Egyptian Old Kingdom, Mycenaean palace states, Western Roman Empire, Classic Maya. The penultimate chapter considers the possible role of inequality as a causal factor in collapse. The final chapter draws some conclusions.

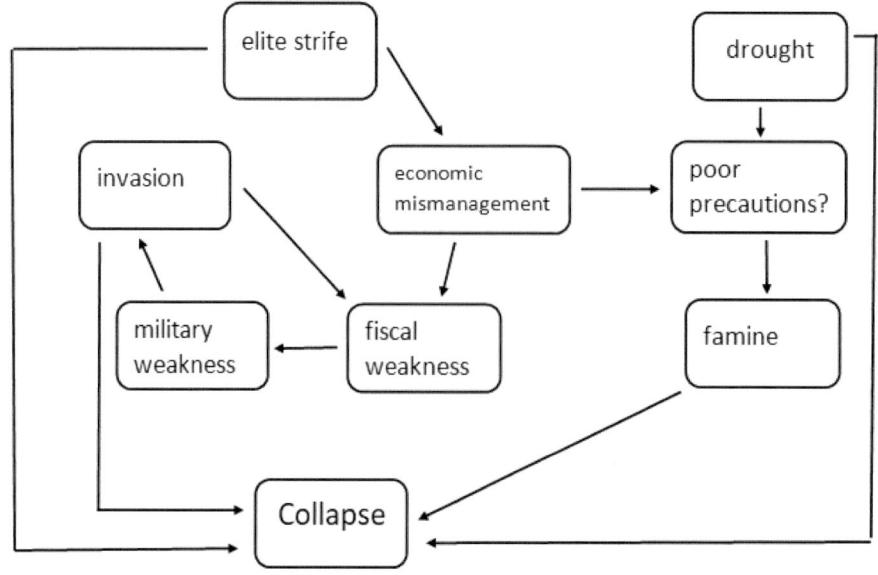

Diagram A: Collapse, Interactive Explanations

III. Egyptian Old Kingdom

During the 'Naqada III' phase (3200-3000 BC) Egypt was united as a large nation state, incorporating the previous Upper and Lower Kingdoms (Bard 2000). What is designated in modern times as the Old Kingdom ran from c 2686 – 2160 BC, a period of consolidation, centralised authority, ruled from Memphis under a series of dynasties (recorded on papyrus now in Turin, the *Turin Canon*). It was a period of massive building projects, notably the pyramids. It collapsed following the death of Pepy II (c 2278-2184 BC) of the Sixth Dynasty ; he reigned for 94 years from the age of 6, (Malek 2000). What followed was described as a 'Dark Age' (Bell 1971) until stability and reunification was re-established in 2055 at the end of the First Intermediate Period.

Kings were believed to have divine status, having been selected by the gods. They ensured stability and protection from external attack; the king was the guarantor of the cycle of seasons, annual flooding of the Nile and hence agricultural and economic stability. Their legitimacy rested on divinity, and these guarantees; the ruling ideology justified their absolute rule, immense wealth: they owned all the country's resources and could requisition labour and could impose taxes (Malek 2000).

Labour needed for the massive construction works was withdrawn from farming (20,000 labourers were needed for the Great pyramid at Giza, Manning 2013) and agriculture was extended to less fertile areas (Kemp 1983 p. 155). The pyramid labour force had to be fed, requiring management of food production and distribution while the construction process itself required management hierarchies and finance from an effective tax system. Thus bureaucratic hierarchies were developed, based on competence rather than royal lineage.

Collapse

A key condition for a stable state is cohesion among the ruling elites. Under Old Kingdom central rule authority was delegated to regional administrations, 'nomes' governed by 'nomarchs'. They were required to maintain irrigation systems, grain storage, public order and tax collection (Malek 2000). The provincial governors were remunerated by royal gifts of sizeable estates. Over time their power, wealth, status, aggrandisement, local royal pretensions all grew, signalled by construction of rich funerary monuments (Middleton 2017 p. 54); some provincial offices became hereditary. They deprived the central treasury of resources because they retained tax revenues destined for the centre and their growing power eroded that of the centre already weakened by the declining authority of the very aged and increasingly enfeebled Pepy II. *'Pepi II's reign was crippled by inaction in the face of crop failures'* (Wilkinson p. 118).. Their acquisition of increasing power became *'unstoppable'* and *'officials were so busy feathering their own nests they neglected the future interests of the Egyptian state'* (Wilkinson 2010 p. 112). They are accused of neglecting key infrastructures including irrigation and farming (Kemp 1983 p. 155, Wilkinson p. 124). *'the fiscal system was probably on the verge of collapse...the ensuing crisis was inevitable ...Central government all but ceased to exist and the advantages of the unified state were lost.'* (Malek, pp. 106-7).

Egypt split into smaller units, returning to the regional situation that had obtained hundreds of years earlier, and prior to formation of the unified state. Separate royal lineages ruled Upper and Lower Egypt. Monumental funerary structures were no longer built, not least because nobody commanded the resources comparable to those of the Sixth Dynasty (Butzer 1980 p. 520, McGuire 1983 p. 113, Seidelmeyer 2000 p. 120).

Bell (1971) writing of a *'Dark Age in Egypt'* told of drought and famine recorded on contemporary tomb inscriptions; her account is echoed by Wilkinson (2010 pp. 124-124), who writes of the breakdown of central authority following the death of Pepi II, causing neglect of irrigation and grain storage but offers no evidence.

An ancient text, *Dialogue of Ipuwer*, seemingly written by a respected eyewitness, tells of lethal attacks on the nobility (Parkinson 1997). *'Noblemen are in distress [commoners] say 'let us suppress the powerful'...the children of princes are dashed against walls...the king has been deposed by the rabble'* (quoted Faulkner 1965 p. 53). Such a picture suggests collapse of asibaya and alienation of commoners from the elite.

However Ipuwer's existence is contentious and his account is said by Van de Mieroop not to be contemporaneous with the collapse (Van de Mieroop, 2011) who also argues that the tomb inscriptions are illegible, that the picture of violence and famine is drawn from inference rather than direct evidence. He points out that text such as that about Ipuwer were later Middle Kingdom constructs expressing exaggerated anxieties of that period (Van De Mieroop pp. 79-85). Even if that were the case it illustrates recognition of the threats posed by inequality, commoner alienation and loss of asibaya.

The scale of collapse is disputed. The tomb inscription of Ankhtifi, a provincial overlord (nomarch) wrote of famine and cannibalism but boasts how, although food was scarce, he never allowed anyone to go hungry in his territory. Maybe, as Middleton (2017 p.59) suggests, this boast was intended to emphasise what a good ruler and manager he was. The motive was to stress *'the people would be helpless without their rulers'* (Seidelmayer 2000 p. 120), that is, we might suppose, to bolster their legitimacy. We have no means of testing this explanation.

Seidelmayer (2000) cautions against seeing the end of the Old Kingdom as initiating a Dark Age. This is in contradiction of Bell (1971). He argues that the emphasis in most of the literature on kings and capitals and their travails overlooks what was going on in the provinces and among the mass of the population. *'...archaeological and epigraphic data indicate a thriving culture among the poorer levels of society'* (Seidelmayer, 2000 p. 112). Moreover *'Provincial governors had 'kept a growing amount of food for use within the provinces themselves...Rural Egypt became economically richer and culturally more complex'* Seidelmayer, op cit).

One may conclude first that there is no consensus about the social and economic severity of the Old Kingdom political collapse.

Explanations of collapse

Possible reasons for collapse of the Old Kingdom are implied by previous discussion, including tension between the centre and provincial elites: *'The policy of promoting provincial elites contained within itself the seeds of destruction of central power'* (Baud op.cit.p.78); inequality and loss of asibaya were also present.

Although provincial territories seem to have thrived (Seidelmeyer), the picture Bell painted, derived from tomb inscriptions, cannot wholly be dismissed. It included famine, mass deaths, cannibalism, and violence caused by *'widespread, severe and prolonged drought'* (Bell, 1971 p.2). She also claims that a more serious factor was a fall in Nile flooding, needed for irrigation, due to drought in Ethiopia from where the Nile flowed (she provides no evidence for this). Representations of desert fauna and trees have been noted on tombs (Kemp). Krom and colleagues (2002) examined fluctuations in Nile Delta sedimentation and found evidence of severe aridity when the Old Kingdom fell (Krom et.al. 2002). Analysis of pollen in the Nile Delta Burullus Lagoon (Bernhardt et.al.2012) was interpreted as indicating reduced flow and periodic serious drought.

Drought would have destroyed royal legitimacy, protection from drought being a symbol of divine approval of the kings, caused economic and fiscal decline and violence as the starving attacked grain stores. Ipuwer described violent uprisings against the nobility, indicating internal strife (Parkinson op.cit), but, as noted earlier, Ipuwer's account is contentious as is his very existence.

Seidelmeyer (2000 op. cit. p. 129) queries the evidence of collapse and argues that any drier conditions would have induced adaptation to lower levels of flooding and *'these climatic changes showed no signs of affecting pharonic civilization'*. Moeller (2005) reviewed he evidence and concluded *'the evidence of Nile floods trends suggests a long term gradual development to generally drier conditions'* and the First Intermediate Period was not triggered by natural catastrophe. She, like Seidelmeyer, stressed the resilience and adaptability of Egyptian society to new climatic conditions, conditions which need not have caused collapse.

To summarise, several of the types of evidence of collapse noted above (p.12) were displayed by the Old Kingdom's demise: ending of central authority, state fragmentation, reduced investment in monumental and funerary construction and economic decline while others features such as violent deaths of the elite at the hands of commoners, described by Ipuwer, are contentious. Political collapse is beyond dispute. But there is no consensus on the scope and severity of economic and cultural collapse.

As to explanations of collapse, several factors were present including internal strife between elites, especially those governing provinces, and the central royal authority *' ...failure to make adjustments in the relationships between the king and local power bases was perhaps the most important factor in the collapse of central authority'* (Manning 2013). There was also possible strife between social classes. Drought was a contributing factor but its significance by itself is disputed. Failure to manage water resources (irrigation and flood control) and inadequate prudent storage of resources, especially grain, possibly contributed to internal violence. Overall the evidence points to dysfunctionality and systems failure in the face of climatic challenge and the breakdown of central authority.

IV. Mycenaean Palace States

The Mycenaean region embraces the Argolid, Attica, Boeotia, Laconia, Messenia, Mycenae, Thebes and Thessaly. The degree of common ethnicity is unknown and although Linear B was the language of written record it was not necessarily the common spoken language, different languages might have coexisted.

Palace states had emerged by Late Helladic III (from c. 1450 BC), developed from the competing, earlier political centres of Late Helladic II (from c. 1600 BC). Evidence for their emergence includes monumental buildings and administrative matters recorded on clay tablets (Shelmerdine and Bennet 2008 p. 289). The Mycenaean states probably emulated the long established Minoan palace states of Crete. Palace states included Mycenae, Pylos, Thebes and Tiryns. As with Minoan states they evolved from being city states to territorial states (in Trigger's sense, 2003) with hegemony over surrounding territories (Bennett 1999). They appeared to have been ruled by a *wanax* who was also the religious leader (Shelmerdine and Bennet 2008) but the extent of his powers, including law making, is unknown. He was surrounded by an elite class, who enjoyed a rich lifestyle. But some chiefdoms seem to have continued and coexisted with palace states.

Palaces were, in a physical sense, *'substantial architectural complexes with public rooms, prestigious building materials and provision for food storage'* (Wardle 1994). Such architectural features together with Linear B evidence of an administrative role identify Midea, Mycenae, Pylos and Thebes as palaces: a relatively small number.

Their purposes seem to have included royal residences, administrative centres, places for ritual ceremonies and redistributive hubs to which resources flowed for retention by the royal elite, disbursement to suppliers of essentials and luxury goods and to workers(but not redistribution in the modern sense of redistribution to those on low incomes; a better term would be 're-allocation' centres). They were the focus of political, religious, ideological and elite life. Their boundaries of these states are unclear but they embraced some of the surrounding territory: Pylos had hegemony over 2000km2 (Bennet 1999).

Their economic control over the surrounding territory is uncertain. Most economic life probably existed outside the palaces although they were attractive centres of consumption. However Linear B evidence indicates palaces set targets for wool production (Shelmerdine, 2008 p. 173; Killen 1964). Linear B evidence of palace-located craft specialisation and division of labour suggests, in the absence of money and a market economy, *'the palaces themselves played a major entrepreneurial role in the economy'*, at least with regard to some luxury artefacts where the palace authorities controlled production and distribution of revenues in kind to dependent or semi-dependent craftsmen (Killen 2008 p.174). At Knossos the palace *'controlled over 1500 dependent women textile workers' as well as bronze smiths'* (Shelmerdine 2008 p.144). But there is no evidence of palace control over some sectors including pottery and bakery.

The degree of economic inequality is indicated by differences in height: royal skeletons were 6cm longer than commoners (p.26 below). *'Bronze Age society was characterised by the power of the palace and its heavy demands on the general population...Palace elites maintained a very high standard of living at the expense of the general population'* (Van De Mieroop 2010 p. 249). This expropriation of resources was the role of the taxation system and embraced olive oil, honey, textiles and other products including wool (Shelmerdine 2008 p. 146, Killen 2008, for the Linear B evidence.).

Collapse

Around 1200 BC '... *the Mycenaean period came to a dramatic end... The palaces were destroyed and the palace system collapsed never to be rebuilt*' (Deger-Jalkotzy 2008 p. 387). In the Late Bronze Age from the late 13th century BC until the early 12th century destructions occurred at several Mycenaean sites (Deger-Jalkotzty 2008, p.387). The precise chronology is contentious (Middleton 2010 p. 12) but destruction at broadly similar times is accepted (Cline 2014 p. 128). Middleton (2010 p. 12) catalogues the destructions at Iria, Katsingri, Korakou and Mycenae in the Argolid and Corinthia, with abandonments Ayios Stephanos, Berbati, Gonia, Prosymna, Tsoungiza, Zygouries; destruction at Menelaion in Lakonia; destruction at Pylos in Messenia and abandonment at Nichoria; destruction at Tteikhos Dymaion in Achaea; abandonment of Brauron in Attica; destruction in Boetia and Phokis at Gla, Krisa, Orchomenos and Thebes. The evidence of physical destruction is clear.

Drews (1993 p.3) wrote of '*arguably the worst disaster in ancient history*', Cline (2014) of '*The end of civilization*' and Deger- Jalkotzy (2008 p. concluded '*Greek civilization was reduced to the level of prehistory*'.

Potential evidence of collapse includes the fall in the number of sites recorded by Popham (1994) but Middleton points out that Popham's sites were either settlements or cemeteries (Middleton 2017 p. 134). Nonetheless the considerable fall in site numbers indicates severe disruption of some kind. Another indicator of collapse is the absence of evidence of new monumental construction following the palace destructions. Linear B writing vanished, as did fresco painting and luxury artefact making (Sherratt 2001 pp. 214-5).

Population was said to have fallen, partly through emigration, taken to be further evidence of collapse (Iocouvou 1999); Stager (1995) said 25,000 migrated to the Levant, about which Middleton's Doctoral dissertation expresses scepticism (2010) because it would have required a fleet of 250-500 ships, which were unavailable, and because the Mycenaeans lacked the necessary navigational skills.

Pylos never recovered although there is evidence of some rebuilding at Mycenae (French 2010) and at Tiryns (Maran 2010).

However Deger-Jalkotzy wrote, confusingly, of post -collapse '*splendid pottery*' and of the '*vitality and innovation*' of vase making and of skilled bronze smiths (op. cit. pp.397-9). He also argues '*linguistic analysis ... suggests the legacy of Mycenaean poetry was transferred through oral poetry*' to the days of Homer (Deger-Jalkotzy 2008 p.406). Moreover the Greek language and worship of major deities continued. Detailed analysis of the archaeological evidence in Thomatos' doctoral dissertation (Thomatos 2006 p. 259) including pottery, terracotta, figurines, jewellery and weapons leads her to conclude '*LH III was not the beginning of a so-called Dark Age but a period of recovery and increased prosperity*'.

To summarise, the evidence points to the collapse of the palatial state political system but some degree of the continuity of important aspects of Mycenaean civilisation.

Explanations of collapse: Earthquakes

Mycenaean palaces lie in an area prone to earthquakes and the widespread destruction is often attributed to earthquakes: Drews (1993), Kilian (1996), Nur and Cline 2000), French (2002) all attribute the destruction at Mycenae to earthquakes, as does Kilian for the destruction at Tiryns. The supporting evidence for Mycenae includes collapsed walls and buildings at several houses, and the Cult Centre, with evidence of fire and crushed skeletons at some of those sites (Nur and Cline 2000).

However the question is not simply whether seismic shocks caused destruction but also whether the physical destruction produced socio-political collapse of the palace states. Drews (1993 p. 39) is sceptical, noting that there is little evidence of mass casualties or *'city-wide fire'*. Nur and Cline (2000) show that a series of earthquakes stretching over 50 years (1225-1175 BC) was possible, but this period embraced the absence of political collapse in some places. The implication from these researches is that earthquakes might have exacerbated socio-political stresses due to other factors but were probably not sufficient by themselves to explain Mycenaean collapse.

Climate change

Collapse was originally attributed to climate change by Carpenter (1996) who claimed it was a factor in population movements and changes in the Mycenaean areas of Greece although not everywhere else; he hypothesised that wrecking of buildings was done by the starving in search of palatial food stores. This claim of population change and the destruction hypothesis was challenged by Dickinson (1974). Since then evidence of climate change has emerged.

Drake said Carpenter had asserted a sudden, short lived climatic event (2012, p. 1866) which *Drake* said is 'an *unlikely candidate for widespread abandonment of palatal centres'* whereas he had found evidence of long lasting aridity from oxygen isotopes in Israel, pollen material in western Greece and Mediterranean sediment cores which he claimed put such stress on densely populated palace states as to render them unsustainable. Long lasting aridity possibly induced emigration of groups who came to be known as named the Sea People and who became marauders around the eastern Mediterranean. Climate change could have contributed to collapse because '*Climate –influenced drops in food production could have destabilized palace centres resulting in internal uprisings*' (Drake 2012, p. 1866), although he notes that the peak in aridity was centuries after collapse. Kaniewski et. al. (2013) reached similar conclusions, with emigration of the Sea people inducing invasion from the north. That invaders would want to settle in arid areas deserted by the indigenous people seems implausible.

The assumption that population density was so high that higher aridity caused pressure on food supply with which the authorities could not cope is not confirmed by Linear B records which provide no evidence of difficulties with food supplies (Middleton 2017 p. 136) and seems to be contradicted by evidence cited by Deger-Jalkotzy (2008 p.406, citing Kroll 1984) that '*In LH IIIC the quality of grains improved in the Argolid and Messenia and the tree population increased.*'

Moreover As Middleton points out (2017 p.136) estimates for the onset of aridity range from 1250 BC to 1190, a range of sixty years, and if 1250 is right '*the palace states adapted and thrived even as climate change was happening*'.

Explanations other than climate change are criticised because they largely fail to explain why rebuilding did not occur other than in some limited sites. A novel explanation, based on climate change, is provided by Finne and colleagues (2017). Analysis of oxygen and carbon isotopes from a stalagmite in a south west Peloponnese cave showed rising aridity following the destruction of the Palace of Nestor at Pylos which '*probably reduced crop yields and helped erode the basis for reinstituting central authority*'.

Cline (2014 p. 147) recalls that droughts were frequent and ' ...*on their own climate change, drought and famines, even if they influenced social tensions...are not enough to have caused the end of the Late Bronze Age without other factors being involved.*

Decline in foreign trade

The proposition that Mycenaean palace centres thrived economically because of their overseas trading relations and monopoly of the distribution of exotic goods but collapsed when this was disrupted has been suggested by Galaty and Parkinson et.al. (2009). Bilateral trading relations were said to have existed between Mycenae and Egypt, Tiryns with Cyprus, Thebes with Mesopotamia. Mycenae suffered from political collapse in Egypt, whereas Tiryns thrived because so did Cyprus but trade was harassed by the Sea People (Sandars 1978).

Sherratt (2001) argues that trade routes came to bypass Greece as larger ships could sail away from the safety of nearby land and the trade came to be dominated by Cypriot traders.

However the economic importance of trade to the palace economies is unproven. Moreover Egyptian collapse came a century after that of Mycenae. Maran (2009 p.246), reviewing the evidence concludes *'As far as the long-distance trade the Eastern Mediterranean is concerned, at least for the Argolid I...do not see any convincing evidence for a crisis'*. Perhaps some economic weakness resulted from some degree of trade loss but it was probably not the principal factor in collapse.

Warfare techniques

Drews (1993) devotes almost 100 pages to arguing that collapse had a military explanation which by itself was sufficient. Central to his argument is the hypothesis that Greek reliance on chariots in battle exposed them to defeat as they were *'overwhelmed by* [barbarian] *swarming infantries equipped with javelins, long swords and a few pieces of armour'*.

However not only is a single explanation for collapse is implausible, the Greek terrain makes any military reliance on chariots unlikely (as Italian tanks found when Mussolini invaded three thousand years later).

Sea Peoples

Attacks by the *Sea Peoples* were blamed for disrupting trade and land incursions (Sandars 1978). Their existence is recorded in Egyptian texts (Cline 2014 p. 1). Their origins are contentious; possibly they were refugees from the Greek mainland or Crete (Cline 2014 p4). Destructions at coastal sites cannot be proved to be their responsibility but they were *'a convenient scapegoat'* (Cline 2014 p.11). And rather than causing collapse they might have been opportunists taking advantage of weakness due to other factors.

Interstate Mycenaean warfare

Greek mythology recounted the struggles between the rulers of Mycenae and Thebes. Tainter (1988 p.202) assigns a crucial role to hegemonic inter-state warfare in causing their collapse, they *'were locked into competitive spirals, each had to make ever increasing investments in military strength and organisational complexity'* and as the marginal returns on these investments fell, collapse followed.

The explanation in terms of inter-politie wars cannot be proved but it seems consistent with their probable origin in elite competition and could be a sufficient explanation for collapse but it must remain only a hypothesis. However it does not explain the destruction and abandonment of non-palace sites (Deger-Jalkotzy 2008), unless they were treated as collaborators of nearby palaces.

Internal strife

Violent struggle between ruling and aspiring dynasties and elites within each politie is possible, especially if succession was disputed and is a plausible factor in collapse because it weakens the resilience of the politie to meet threats, whether from external enemies, natural disaster or popular uprising. However, while suggested by some (e.g. Dickinson 2006(i) p.54) it remains only conjecture in the absence of evidence other than (Homeric) myth.

Another possibility is uprisings by commoners, especially in the face of famine, if drought was present (a contentious matter as explained p. 18), or in revolt against over-burdensome resource extraction by elites. There is no evidence for this. The evidence needed would include socially differentiated skeletal trauma, a topic that does not appear to have been researched. Such research as has been done seems to have focussed on evidence of ancient Greek dietary habits and evidence of skeletal trauma is contentious, possibly due to clumsy excavation (Voutsaki et. al.2 006).

Rural collapse

A very different explanation of collapse is offered by Maran (2009). Instead of the destruction of palaces that induced collapse it was that of the villages. They were under pressure to provide labour, tributes and supplies to the palaces. Military service reduced agricultural manpower; supplies to the palaces fell; reciprocal palace support declined as they weakened and the whole system imploded it into spreading armed conflicts.

This hypothesis seems to make a reasonable point: if not the cause of collapse, declining rural supplies to the palace centres would have exacerbated their problems.

Systems collapse

Renfrew's analysis of systems collapse (Renfrew 1979) involving a chain reaction and features of collapse noted above (p. 8) appears to match the Mycenaean collapse but it has been criticised by Drew (1993 p. 88) because it does not explain their longevity: they were no more vulnerable in 1200 BC than they had been earlier. He also argues the systems collapse hypothesis cannot explain the physical destruction of the palaces *'the systems collapse hypothesis does not address the essence of the Catastrophe...That essence is not economic or social but physical: the palaces were destroyed'*.

He ignores the fit between the archaeological evidence and Renfrew's model of the features of collapse; instead he focuses on and defines collapse in a very narrow way and advocates military defeat at the hands of invading armies of infantry as *the* cause (see above).

Conclusions

The palace-centred political system, and palaces as architectural constructs collapsed; many features of Mycenaean civilisation especially writing vanished; but the language, religion and some features of material culture survived - traditions not dependent on palatial organisation.

It is clear that explanation of Mycenaean political collapse is especially speculative: the very existence and, if present, the severity of potential explanatory factors is highly contentious because of the inadequacy of archaeological and textual evidence. This is the case with such factors as drought, earthquakes, invasion by Sea peoples, interstate warfare, dynastic and lineal strife, popular uprisings. Any or all of these factors might have had a role to play. But scepticism over their presence makes explanation exceptionally conjectural unlike, say, the collapse of the Roman Empire where the debate is over the relative contributions of various internal and external factors rather than their existence.

V. The Western Roman Empire

The Western Roman Empire (WRE) was created in the late Third century CE when Emperor Diocletian divided the Roman Empire into western and eastern parts to enhance the effectiveness of governance. He judged the empire, covering the area east from the Atlantic seaboard to the Euphrates and south from the Antonine Wall to the Sahara, was too widely spread and diverse for rule from one centre of authority. He established a tetrarchy: each part was ruled by its own Augustus, each of whom had a Caesar as deputy. It is unclear whether this decision should be praised for aiming to improve administration, although it increased bureaucratic and military costs, or regarded as a source of enduring internal rivalry and conflict. The ERE lasted until 1453 when Constantinople was taken by the Ottoman Turks.

The lifespan of the WRE is contentious. The quest for an end date implies an event but the decline and ending of the WRE was a drawn out process, initiated by the defeat at Hadrianople in 376 of Emperor Valens by the Goths, which signalled declining Roman power to the its neighbours. An end date of 410, when Rome was sacked by Visigoths led by Alaric *'is commonly given'* (Middleton 2017 p. 194) although there was no mass destruction and little changed. The *'official date'* (Tainter 1988 p. 148) of 476 is another candidate, when the last emperor of Roman lineage, Romulus Augustus, was persuaded to renounce his title and authority by the Roman army commander of Gothic ancestry, Odoacer, with the tacit consent of the eastern Emperor Zeno; Odoacer took over rule of the WRE, the emperors of which *'had long been controlled by barbarian generals'* anyway (Boardman et.al. 1986, p.810). Bowerstock (1991 p. 31) calls 476 a *'literary conceit'*. A different perspective was that of Henri Pirenne who viewed the Mediterranean as central to Roman civilisation and dominance, which ended in the seventh century with the creation of Arab dominance, a view endorsed by Moorhead (2001 p.274). Barbarian incursions in the west were temporarily reversed by the campaigns of Justinian (ERE Emperor) 535-554 but the Lombards invaded successfully and the WRE was dismantled over the following century.

The WRE was dismembered by an interrupted process of invasions by peoples who established their own authority over the territories they invaded and occupied, which Rome was unable to prevent. Table A summarises the chronology of dismemberment.

Table 2. Barbarian Invasions

Mid 3rd Century AD	Territories in Dacia and between Danube and Rhine relinquished
355	Cologne sacked
376	Tervingi allowed to settle
378	Rome defeated at Hadrianople
401	Alaric attacked Rome
406/7	Vandals, Suevi, Alans crossed Rhine
407	Germanic groups attacked Gaul, enter Spain
410	Alaric sacked Rome
412	Germanic invaders took over Spain
413	Visigoths settled in southern Gaul
439	Visigoths crossed from Spain to Africa
439	Visigoths took Carthage
446	Plea from Briton for help rejected
445	Vandals sacked Rome
468	Combined ERE-WRE army defeated by Vandals
568	Lombards invade then rule Italy until defeated by Franks.

Based on Goffart (1980), Heather (2005), Middleton (2017)

What Collapsed?

There is considerable documentary evidence of the decline and eventual collapse of the WRE : Middleton (2017) indicates secondary sources while Heather (1985 pp. 537-8) lists major primary sources. Archaeological evidence is to be found in the form of the remains of ruined fortifications and other structures and artefacts scattered throughout the empire. Storey and Storey (2017 pp. 40-47) list almost 100 examples of archaeological evidence of '*disjuncture*', which '*serve as harbingers of the end.*' They emphasise site abandonment identified by surveys across the empire and reject explanations in terms of nucleation, for which they say no evidence exists (Storey and Storey 2017 p. 50). Archaeological evidence of a drop in living standards reinforces the picture (Ward Perkins discussed below). But what was it that collapsed? Was there a collapse?

Gibbon wrote of decline and fall to a Dark Age but 'transformation' became the conventional wisdom followings Brown's lead (Brown 1971). The contrasting paradigms are illustrated by titles such as *The Awful Revolution* (Wallbank 1969) and *The Transformation of the Roman World* (European Science Foundation).

That the WRE was dismantled as a centralised political authority over Western Europe, the Balkans and North Africa is beyond doubt. By around 490 Britain had been abandoned, and the departing Roman forces established a Breton Kingdom, Iberia and north Africa were controlled by Visigoths whose territory covered Gaul south and west of the Loire; a Frankish kingdom extended from the Rhine to the Loire; and Burgundians and Alans occupied southeast Gaul (Heather 1985 p. 471).

For Bowerstock (1996 p. 32) Rome did not fall in the fifth or sixth centuries, it was '*a period of transformation and change*' because the ERE was flourishing and he asserted '*no responsible historian ...would want to address or acknowledge the fall of Rome as fact or paradigm.*' Halsall (2007 p. 21) wrote 'it *is fair to say that the transformation approach is the current paradigm.*' This paradigm derives from Brown's 1971 *The World of Late Antiquity*. He acknowledged that '*Italy became a geographical expression*' (p. 131) and that even Rome realised that the '*centre of gravity had slipped ...to the Eastern Mediterranean*' (p.176). But his thrust was to emphasise the cultural creativity of Byzantium and the consolidation of Christianity – leading to '*the social and spiritual revolution of the Late Antique period*' (p. 9). His focus of concern was the continuation and cultural transformation of the Roman Empire in the East, which hardly denies the collapse of the Western Empire, which was political: Tainter's criterion for collapse (p. 10 above).

The traditional perception of collapse was restated by Ward-Perkins (2005) on the basis of careful archaeological research. He infers a steep fall in living standards (pp. 13-310) from the use of wooden pieces rather than ceramic roof tiles, wooden rather than stone house construction, a decline in pottery standards (p. 104) and a decline in economic complexity to below pre-Roman times (pp. 117-120), and declining population (pp. 138). He argues that Barbarian violence was a reality and life must have been '*very unpleasant*'. Data from Arctic ice cores indicate that copper, iron and sliver smelting fell to pre-Roman levels.

Loss of tax revenue from loss of territory had serious implications for the military budget. Heather (1985 p. 297) says Roman historians estimated that the army accounted for '*about two-thirds of... revenues*', which is consistent with Storey and Storey's 2017 estimates (op.cit. p. 84). Therefore loss of revenue meant drastic cuts to the military budget in the absence of other major expenditures to cut. He estimated that loss of revenue from North Africa alone implied a cut of 40,000 infantrymen or 20,000 cavalry (p. 296) on top of earlier cuts. This implies weaker ability to resist further barbarian encroachment.

To summarise, claims of a thriving civilisation in Byzantium cannot deny political collapse of the WRE as an overarching political structure stretching from the Atlantic to the Euphrates and from Scotland to the Sahara. Real damage to living standards seems to have accompanied political failure. The loss of territory and the consequential cut in tax revenues and hence military power set in train a cycle of positive feedback.

What caused collapse?

Several explanations for collapse have been proposed. Demandt (1984, cited by Bowerstock op.cit.) listed 210, although many were synonyms for one another or contradictory. Possible reasons include the rise of Christianity, Barbarian incursions, internal strife, natural disasters, economic problems, failure of the ERE to provide military help and costly complexity.

Christianity

Christianity as a cause of collapse has been associated with Gibbon who wrote (p. 437) that the clergy *'preached patience and pusillanimity...and the last remains of military spirit were buried'* while internal tension was exacerbated by religious factionalism. Although he credits the church for holding society together he says *'it had some influence on the decline and fall of the Roman Empire'* (p. 436) but concluded *'the most potent cause of destruction was the domestic hostilities of the Romans themselves.'* (p.722). The rise of Christianity was neither a sufficient nor a necessary explanation of collapse for which more plausible explanations exist.

Barbarians

The name and image of 'Barbarian' implies an uncouth savage but is derived from Roman contempt for *'Lesser breeds without the law'* (Kipling, *Recessional*) and not necessarily reality. Many were Christians, albeit Arians (regarded as heretics) and some rose to great power in the Roman army and politically. St Augustine wrote that the sacking of Rome involved less savagery than shown by the Romans in their conquests (*City of God* (I, 15).

Bronson (1988 p. 201) convincingly argues that although often present at collapse Barbarians did not necessarily cause it but were exploiting opportunities for acquiring booty and land in states that were already weakening for internal reasons. As for Alaric's sack of Rome in 410, MacMullen (1990 p. 204) reminds us that *'He and his men were Romans'* and his aim was loot not destruction of the empire. Pohl (2005 p. 464) claims that much of the physical destruction of Italy is attributable to Justinian's campaign to recapture it rather than to the Barbarian occupiers.

The first mass Barbarian invasion was in 376 when about 20,000 Tervingi (Goths) fleeing the Huns were allowed by Emperor Valens to cross the Danube into Roman territory. They were seen as potential farmers of under-exploited land, a source of tax revenue and as army recruits. They were promised food and shelter which was not delivered by commanders on the ground (Halsall p. 186, Heather p. 376. Whether their needs had been underestimated or corrupt officers and officials appropriated supplies to sell at extortionate prices is uncertain. When other Goths invaded , Greuthungi, the Tervingi joined them and defeated the Roman army at Hadrianople in 378, killing Valens who had not waited for his nephew Gratien's reinforcements; the latter massacred many Goths but eventually peace was restored and they were allowed to settle. Valens was jealous of Gratien's record of success and failure to wait for him support was a fatal instance of intra-elite rivalry. Hadrianpole was a key indicator of Rome's emerging military weakness. Allowing Goths to settle on Roman territory was the first step towards dismemberment of the WRE.

Barbarian recruitment into the Roman army was long established: *'the predominance of barbarians in Constantine's expeditionary force of 311/2 allowed him to extend his rule over Italy'* (MacMullen 1988 p. 201) and *'probably more than half'* Theodosius' forces assembled to fight the pretender Eugenius were barbarian (MacMullen op.cit. p. 204). Barbarian soldiers were used against other barbarians and even by Roman rivals as with Constantine's attack on Julian in 361 (Halsall op.cit. p. 149).

Loss of territory to barbarians was prolonged and extensive. In the mid Third century Rome gave up territory between the Danube and the Rhine as well as Dacia (Halsall p. 138) and, as described on page

23 above, outside Italy the WRE came under barbarian control by 490, which Rome was unable to resist. They seized opportunities to exploit Rome's weakness and Rome had little choice but to adapt to this, apart from Justinian's re-conquests which did not endure. The loss of territory, revenue and military budgets was a cumulative vicious circle: barbarians certainly dismembered the WRE but this raises the question of why Rome was unable to resist them before this cycle started.

One possibility is that the Roman army was too small in the first place. Heather (p. 446) puts the size of the army as at least 300,000 in 375 against total barbarian forces on all fronts at about 120,000. But the Roman forces were composed of semi-autonomous armies the soldiers of which were loyal to their own commander. Many were garrison forces in towns and with a local focus and untrained for battlefields. So the relevant Roman force was not 300, 000 but *'At the onset of the crisis the western field army probably numbered ...80,000 men'* and in particular battles they might have been outnumbered. But numbers are not everything and MacMullen (1988 pp. 273-274) emphasises poor equipment and rations, attributable to corruption. And as for the vicious circle of territorial/revenue/army budget losses, it was possible, in principle, to raise tax rates to compensate for the shrinking tax base but this did not happen - presumably for political reasons about which one can only speculate. One possibility is that Diocletian's earlier tax increases has exhausted any appetite for shouldering yet higher burdens among elites and commoners alike. Moreover loss of territory, and hence part of the tax base, to the barbarian invaders limited the scope for raising more revenue. Bronson's argument (Bronson 1988) that barbarians are not necessarily the root cause of the death of the WRE needs to face two counter arguments. One is that it is oversimplified because the barbarian dismemberment of the WRE is beyond doubt but was facilitated by domestic failure to meet the conditions needed for stability. The second is the possibility that they outnumbered the army.

It can be argued that the Western Empire had its own agency in the creation of the barbarian challenge. The empire contributed to the coalescence of the Germanic threat in particular, in two ways. First, as was its custom, it selected a local leader with whom to deal. This enhanced his status and power among his neighbours over whom he established hegemony, leading to a larger group. Second, the aggressive expansionary efforts of the WRE induced alliances among those it threatened. Thus *'The Roman Empire had sown the seeds of its own destruction...not because of internal weakness... By virtue of its unbounded aggression Roman Imperialism was ultimately responsible for its own destruction.'* Heather pp. 458). This stresses barbarian invasion induced by Roman power rather than internal Roman weakness.

Failure of the Eastern Empire to help

Gibbon (p.436) lays part of the blame for collapse on what he alleges was the failure of the Eastern Empire to provide military support because it welcomed the weakening of a rival. This is disputed by Heather (p. 388) who argues that Constantinople was preoccupied with threats from Persia and from the Huns but nonetheless sent 4000 men to help in 410 who secured Ravenna. Further help and joint operations continued.

Internal strife

The Roman Empire had a history of peasant uprisings, and violent intra-elite internal strife. There were frequent civil wars 75-250, six emperors in 238; expensive foreign wars, barbarian incursions, price inflation, and internal violence all threatened collapse averted by supplementing public finances by currency debasement and higher taxes (MacMullen 1990 passim). Diocletian's reforms involved still higher unpopular, regressive taxation and higher bureaucratic and military costs due to the division of the Empire. Constantine decreed (322) that they be tied to their estate, virtual serfdom, and their legal rights were curtailed (Wallbank 1969). Of course, inequality preceded Diocletian: Scheidel (2017, p. 77) describes extreme inequality in the second century BCE. Unfortunately we have no time series of measures of Roman inequality (or, at least, nobody has assembled it) but some textual evidence suggests it became more unbearable. According to Salvian, (a fifth century presbyter at the Marseilles church), peasants were reduced to starvation levels and were imprisoned if they could not pay their tax and either sold their land or sold their children into slavery. Many peasants *'migrated to the Goths or the Bacaudae'* (*marauding* groups) (Robinson 1904). Salvian's account was treated with scepticism by Grey (2006) although Mazzarino (1966 p. 65) quotes fifth century Zosimus saying the same thing. It seems plausible that commoner alienation, huge inequality, loss of asibaya, elite selfishness and intra-elite strife all contributed to eroding the conditions necessary for a stable, functioning state.

Corruption was rife; administration was *'primitive... it was a ramshackle edifice'* (Heather op.cit. p. 439). The last five WRE Emperors averaged fewer than two years with the last, Romulus Augustus serving under a year before being deposed by Odoacer. In short, popular alienation if not outright violence, absence of elite cohesion including a common strategy all suggest a state close to collapse, for which Barbarian invasion was the catalyst if not the fundamental cause.

Economic factors

The WRE economy was predominantly agricultural and labour intensive. But the Mediterranean climate is characterised by low average rainfall and the risks of both periodic aridity and torrential rain. So the agricultural base is at risk from climatic threats, which periodically damaged output and hence tax revenue which was primarily based on farm output. The main input being labour any migration from the land would have hit output and tax revenue. Constantine's 322 decree implies this was a threat but Heather (op. cit. pp.114-115) is sceptical about desertion of the land although the burden of taxation would have rendered farming of marginal land at least uneconomic and his assertion is problematic. The military budget, taking perhaps two- thirds of public finance was especially exposed to fluctuating and falling revenue in any economic/agricultural decline and Odoacer was so concerned at falling morale and loyalty due to poor pay that he sought army support by redistributing land to the soldiery from landlords. Restricted budgets led, over many years, to recruitment of Barbarians into the army, with the risk of falling quality and loyalty but, *post hoc ergo propter hoc* apart as an explanation for defeats, there appears to be no robust evidence for this.

Along the lines of Tainter's reasoning, it can be argued that the expansion of the bureaucracy following Diocletian's administrative reforms induced rising marginal costs but diminishing returns because of the division of the Empire, which also put strains on the budget and hence military capacity. In short, a combination of the sensitivity of tax revenue to falling agricultural/ economic activity plus the negative administrative marginal cost/benefit ratio lead Storey and Storey (op. cit p.85) to conclude that *'circumstances and a multi-factorial array of challenges did make economic collapse perhaps the most crucial of factors in the equation of collapse.'*

Natural Disasters

Plague as a cause of agricultural decline or disaster through its impact on the agricultural labour force is a little explored issue, unmentioned by Heather or Middleton and touched on by Storey and Storey. Wagner et al. (2006) refer to Procopius' speculative claim that 'Justinian's Plague' killed 100 million, which would have had a devastating economic effect but, being medical researchers, they offer no economic analysis while Little's *Plague and the End of Antiquity* (Little K, Ed. 2006) misses the opportunity completely. Storey and Storey (op. cit. p.183) suggest it put an end to Justinian's attempt to retake the WRE which, if correct, must count as a major explanation in its collapse.

Climate change combined with human action is another under explored issue although not so neglected as plague. Soil erosion due to deforestation and over exploitation of the land was estimated by Judson (1968) to have risen tenfold in Central Italy, with negative implications for the productivity and yield of the land and the economy. Tainter and Crumley (2007) regard the cooling of Europe after 300 as contributing to agricultural decline and exacerbating political stress. Later a severe climate event, associated with a massive although distant earthquake, is said by Procopius (cited Storey and Storey p. 182) to have blotted out the sun for a year in 536-7. As they assert (p. 184), the implications of climate change for collapse needs to be explored systematically.

Conclusions

The WRE was dismantled while the ERE survived for another 1000 years, leading some (e.g. Brown) to query the notion of the collapse of the Roman Empire. This misses the point: the WRE as a political and imperial entity collapsed, although aspects of Roman civilisation continued especially in Byzantium.

The role of the Barbarians in the collapse is best seen in a dynamic context: ineffective governance associated with incompetence, corruption, dynastic instability and intra-elite strife, induced economic and fiscal weakness, smaller military budgets and capacity which encouraged barbarian incursions hence loss of territory and a reduced tax base and further military decline. Earlier WRE aggressive expansion seeded barbarian reaction and cohesion and counter attacks. The cost of the bureaucracy and military overheads grew following the WRE-ERE division and strained the budget under pressure from loss of territory and fighting the invaders. The alienated peasantry seem to have collaborated with the invaders in some places while the Bacaudae revolts tied down soldiers sent to defeat them. All this amounts to a dynamic systems collapse. The role of adverse climate change in damaging agriculture and the economy and the impact of plague in aborting Justinian's efforts to re-establish the WRE are both themes warranting further investigation.

The collapse graphically illustrates failure to meet the conditions needed for stability: effective defence against external attack, robust public finances, intra-elite cohesion, a society-wide spirit of asibaya, commoner and elite acceptance of the legitimacy of the ruling regime, including willingness to support the state in the face of external attack.

VI. Classic Mayan collapse

The Classic Mayan period c. 300-900 AD had city based polities which competed and sometimes cooperated. A common civilisation and culture is demonstrated its writing, pottery, architecture, kingly divinity, and calendar, together with an elite, hierarchical social, political and administrative structure. They varied in size and functions but *'they all share enough in common to constitute a city-state culture'* (Hutson S. 2016, p. 68). Detailed examination of fine obsidian, jade, shell and stone artefacts indicates the presence of craft specialisation catering for elite customers Moholy-Nagy (1994).

The Classic Mayan period is conventionally divided (Demarest 2004) into:

- Early classic 300-600 AD
- Late classic 600- 800
- Terminal classic 800-1000
- Early post classic 1000-1150
- Mid post classic 1150-1350
- Late post classic 1350-1500

Mayan writing was deciphered forty years ago and is found as inscriptions on monuments and stelae often recording the (alleged) achievements of kings in warfare. The chronologies of kings were recorded in such inscriptions. Violent warfare was common between rival states although they sometimes formed unstable alliances. Major city states such as Tikal had hegemony over other cities but they tended to fragment into smaller states that expanded, such as Dos Pilos, which later collapsed. Interpretation of inscriptions on monuments and stellae suggest the number of Maya cities peaked around 800AD (Morley, 1946, cited Webster 2002, p.183).

Collapse

Little Mayan documentation that might help to explain the causes of collapse remain, largely having been destroyed by Friar Diego de Landa in the sixteenth century while his own account is suspect (Landa 1566/1978).

Gann and Thompson suggest (1931, cited Webster p.185) that population fell as cities were abandoned and arts were subject to *'catastrophically sudden extinction.'* Interpretation of inscriptions on monuments and stellae suggest the number of Maya cities peaked around 800 AD (Morley 1946 cited by Webster 2002 p. 183). The political and administrative structure along with elite material culture collapsed into the Terminal classic c. 750 -1050 AD (Demarest et. al 2004). *'After the population crash at the end of the Late Classic Period it appears that elite residents were replaced by commoners. By the end of the Terminal Classic elite status goods were no longer produced.'* (Moholy-Nagy 1994 p. 66; Webster 2002 pp. 183-4). Urban populations fell as cities were abandoned (Gann and Thompson 1931, cited Webster p. 185), arts were subject to *'catastrophically sudden extinction'* (Proskouriakov, cited Webster 2002).

However the above picture is oversimplified. Cities did not completely vanish, chronologies were subject to lengthy gaps and some cities had no chronological inscriptions, although gaps in dates on monuments and stellae did not necessarily indicate anything about site occupation (Webster 2002, p. 186, pp. 202-4). City cultures were not as similar as once believed: northern and southern centres had different architectural styles. Some, like Caracol were less hierarchical than other (Chase, Chase and Smith 2009 p.176). Ceramic evidence suggests settlements continued after abandonment of some major centres (Webster 2002 p. 8).

Aimers (2011) argues that archaeological evidence indicates that site abandonment was spread over several centuries, from Petexbatun in the mid eighth century AD, mid eleventh century at Chichen Itza, and 1697 at Tayasal. Aimer regards this as indicating lengthy decline rather than collapse. As Webster argues (2002 p. 186) although Maya centres collapsed at different times '...they were all equally vulnerable.'

As there was no Mayan state it is appropriate to think in terms of the collapse of individual Mayan states, and that Mayan civilisation was maintained over a lengthy period while particular states collapsed.

Causes of collapse

Barbarian invasions and destruction of the civilisation responsible for the pyramids were popular nineteenth century explanation of collapse with white explorers and adventurers, who contrasted the magnificent Mayan monuments with the simple lives of the local native population who were deemed unlikely to have been descended from that civilisation. But large structures, stellae and possible embryonic *'glyphs and numerals'* had appeared by 400 BC and by *'By 100 AD the fundamental building blocks of complex Maya y culture were firmly in place'* (Webster2002, pp. 44-45). So the Classic structures of c. 800 had ancient roots and if the product of invaders why did they and their culture disappear?

Sudden, widespread disaster around 800 AD was suggested by Proskouriakoff in 1946 (cited Webster 2002 p. 186). However the number of cities with recordings of dates declined but did not disappear nor collapse at the same time (Webster 2002) and there are gaps in chronologies at several sites that possibly reflect small collapses ('hiatuses'); the gap at Tikal had a gap from 562 until 692 AD, a gap of 130 years (Webster 2002, p.192).

Climate Change, Drought

Catastrophic climate change, excessive rainfall or droughts have been common and popular explanations of Mayan collapse. Isotopes from the shells of freshwater snails in Yucatan have revealed significant climatic variability (Gunn et. al. 2002). Spanish invaders recorded droughts and massive rainfall as do surviving Mayan records of Chilam Balams (Gunn et. al., op. cit.). Gunn and colleagues (2002 p.80) found that differences between wetness and dryness could occur not only within years but for decades, with no dry season at all in some years and the pattern varied from place to place.

Landa (cited by Middleton 2017 p. 254) writing in the sixteenth century recorded conflicts over water, town abandonment and death rates approaching fifty percent due to famine brought on by drought. Gill (2000) strongly advocated a long lasting climatic and demographic 'mega drought' catastrophe as the cause of collapse, which produced millions of deaths due to famine. Evidence for drought exists: e.g. analysis of lake sediment cores in Yucatan (Haug et. al. 2003) concluded *'our data show a clear link between the chronology of regional drought and the demise of Classic Maya culture'*. Other studies that found an association between collapse and drought include Curtis et. al. 2001, Hodell et. al.2005 and Gill 2007.

Although an apocalyptic mega drought is largely not accepted as the explanation for Mayan collapse, droughts are recognised as contributing to Mayan collapse, subject to important caveats.

Gill's mega drought hypothesis has been rejected by Demarest (2004) who found critical flaws in Gill's analysis including selective use of unrelated data, a jumble of theories with no testable theoretical rationale. Lake sediment cores from Yucatan were from locations near cities that did not collapse but thrived 750-1000 AD. Rainfall in northern Yucatan was half that at Copan which collapsed early; some places like Tikal, without access to water such as rivers lasted longer than some that had no such access.

Aimers (2011) argues that climate scientists ignore droughts that happened in times of growth and assign no agency to Mayan capacity for reacting to challenges although he offers no evidence of such resilience. Hodell (2011), an earth scientist, warns that proxies for historic rainfall such as lake and marine sediment cores are subject to uncertainties including dating and chronologies. He advises that the furtheraway is a sample taken from the Mayan lowlands the less it can tell is with confidence about lowland rainfall. He questions what a rainfall record from the Cariaco Basin can tell us about precipitation at Tikal, 2700kms away.

A further consideration is that dating of droughts and collapse are each fraught with error so that ostensible temporal correlation between the two will be subject to even larger margins of error; comparing climate and archaeological data is therefore subject to uncertainty.

Wahl (2008) investigated oxygen isotopes at Peten and found evidence of dry conditions but pollen counts indicated that agriculture and settlement continued. He suggests that some degree of dryness suited Mayan agriculture. The 2014 symposium on Mayan drought (Iannone Ed.) concluded that drought occurred without a common collapse, responses varied across sites and regions, and it stressed Mayan terrain varied considerably: mountains, rainforests, , lowland plains, deep river valleys and dry plains so that a single mega drought is not a plausible.

Internal and external strife and violence

Violent conflict between and within states is recognised as a possible factor in any collapse. Violent intra-elite and dynastic competition was rife. Political conflicts in the Petexbatun region lasted a century from the late seventh century (Demarest 2004 pp.257-60). It involved violence and instability, population decline and agricultural disruption. Warfare was common between aggrandising rival rulers seeking bigger territories, between rival dynasties and their followers, and between rulers and ambitious elites. (Demarest 2014 p.190). Detailed study of destructions and defacements are attributed by Moholy-Nagy to ritual destruction by rival lineages: 'lowland *Maya socio-political structures were unstable, intense chronic factionalism may have been the normal state of affairs'* (Moholy-Nagy, 2016 pp.258-260). For example Chichen – Itza collapsed following violent rivalry between siblings (Webster 2002 p.205)

Instability, depopulation and agricultural decline set in followed by collapse. Fash (1991) suggests this was the fate of Copan. For Demarest collapse proceeded in phases. Dos Pilos was founded in 650 by members of Tikal's royal family but with support from Calakmul, Tikal's main rival. This support declined as Calakmul's power weakened. Dos Pilos went into decline; temple and palace walls were broken to provide stone for defensive walls but Dos Pilos was abandoned in 761. Aguateros experienced population growth in the eighth century but was attacked and destroyed c. 800-830.

In summary, collapse was that of a political system including the end of royal rule, and it embraced depopulation, the end of a material culture and of new public architecture. It was more gradual in some locations than others. The causes are complex and their relative importance probably varied from place to place, with periodic drought (but not a single megadrought,) interstate warfare and internal violence all having roles. The necessary conditions for stability were absent, especially intra-elite cohesion.

VII. Inequality

Inequality and state collapse

The assertion that inequality is a source of civil strife within states was asserted by Aristotle (Politics, Book 5) and De Tocqueville, (1835, p.302) who saw it as a factor in all revolutions. But there has been no systematic study of what contribution, if any, inequality made to the collapse of ancient states (Levitt, 2019). Middleton (2017, p. 341) acknowledges the roles of fairness and inclusiveness in supporting stability and, implicitly, the converse but does not explore the issue further.

Studies of the relationship between inequality and civil strife in modern states (Muller 1985, Lichbach 1989, Hibbs 1973, Boix 2004, Collier and Hoefler2004, McCulloch 2005, Buhaug 2011) reveal no consensus on concerning inequality as an explanation but the following issues emerge that are relevant to ancient states:

i. grievance may arise because of economic inequality and may be a necessary condition for violent civil disorder and revolt but alone it is not sufficient;

ii. leadership and organisation are necessary to transpose grievance into effective action;

iii. inequality may not be economic alone; ethnicity may be associated with feelings of grievance (horizontal inequality) and can be a source of group cohesion and leadership and was a feature of the Goth defeat of the Roman army at Hadrianpole in 378 CE;

iv. grievance-fuelled uprisings may be repressed by the authorities for a time but not necessarily indefinitely;

v. disaffection by the military, dissatisfied elites, and rivalry between competing dynasties and elites have the potential to dismember central authority and these were factors in the collapse of the Old Kingdom Sixth Dynasty, the WRE and the Maya, and the Mycenaean city states if legend is to be believed.

Inequality and violence in ancient states.

Perhaps the earliest evidence of ancient inequality inducing violence is that suggested by Muller and colleagues (2015). Their research at Okoliste in today's Bosnia-Herzogovina, founded c. 5100 BC, found that larger houses, A and C, had evidence of cereal grinding and weaving equipment on a scale greater than that, if any, of their neighbours: house A had four times the cereal processing capacity as their neighbours, which they took to imply dominance of supply. Around 4800 BCE both houses A and C seem to have been subject to destruction by arson, which Muller et. al. take to indicate violent action by the less well off.

Formidable architectural constructions such as palaces and pyramids signal gross inequality between kings and the mass of the population and Gini estimates of interpersonal economic inequality, based on house sizes, are quoted *Ten Thousand Years of Inequality* (2018, Kohler and Smith). Boix and Rosenbluth suggest height as a proxy for Egyptian economic inequality: the heights of male mummies dated c. 1500 BCE are 166.2 cms. but the height of commoners was 157.0 cms. At Mycenae they estimated the height of royal males as 172.5 cms. whereas commoners were over 6 cms. shorter. Scheidel (2017, pp. 264-9 and passim) documents immense inequality in the Roman Empire) and the Republic before that). Estimates of several Maya Gini coefficients of inequality were published by Hutson (2016 p. 156).

So ancient inequality is beyond doubt but what did this imply for violence and state collapse?

The account by Ipuwer of attacks on the nobility by the Egyptian poor has been disputed (p. 12 above.) But it is plausible that food riots and attacks on grain stores maintained by royal palaces and elites broke out in times of drought- induced famine. However such acts of violence do not necessarily imply a political aim of state destruction, although they might have been a contributory factor.

Internal class-based strife in Mycenaean states was suggested by Hooker (1976) who claimed that the lower strata speaking a Dorian Greek dialect revolted against the elite, prompted by drought-induced famine. Drought is a possibility but there is no evidence for the existence of a Dorian, or any other class-based revolt. (One avenue for examining this would be an analysis of possible socially differentiated skeletal trauma, with bone length and tooth health as class markers). But a breakdown in civil order, class based or not, is possible if the Mycenaean states were collapsing for other reasons.

Inequality and violence were certainly features of the Western Roman Empire although some dispute the evidence. Salvian, a fifth century presbyter at the Marseilles church wrote *'The many are oppressed by the few...many migrate to the Goths or the Bacaudae'* (roving violent groups, predominantly of peasant origin) (Robinson1904) However Grey, (20060 is sceptical about Salvian's claims and argues Salvian's motive was to criticise the Unchristian profligacy and corruption of the rich. But Mazzarino (1996, p. 65) attributes similar accounts of peasants joining the barbarians to the fifth century commentator Zosimus.

'Bacaudae' (alternatively 'Bagaudae') is the label attached to participants in peasant revolts. Thompson (1952) reviewed their history. They originated in the second or third century CE and in their early activities were led and organised by a former Roman soldier, Maternus, and their title was attached to similar revolts over succeeding centuries, when members of the alienated poor joined the Bacaudae or collaborated with the invading barbarians. *'They reached such a climax in the first half of the fifth century as to be almost continuous'* (Thompson p. 20).

However Thompson's thesis has been challenged. Couper and Howe (2016) argue that it is unlikely that class consciousness existed among the Roman peasantry and that their grievances were the consequence of a fall in living standards, resulting from economic downturn, rather than class enmity (or, in the provinces such as Gaul and Spain, by any notion of nationalism). But in a time of falling living standards for the many who believed that their suffering was not shared by the better off, the distinction may be true but trivial. Van Dam (1985) claims that their objective was not state collapse but reform. But the story of the Bacaudae reveals considerable resentment at inequality and the degree of alienation of commoners from the state, which they were unwilling to defend, or were prepared to attack by involvement in the Bacaudae or even through collaboration with 'barbarian' invaders.

Evidence of popular resentment

Textual evidence of popular revolt induced by inequality embraces that of Ipuwer in the Egyptian Old Kingdom, which is contentious, and that of Salvian and Zosimus in the Western Roman Empire. Archaeological evidence is sparse but includes destruction of large houses at Okoliste; attacks on elite Minoan, Mycenaean and Mayan structures and inscriptions. Driessen (2013 p. 121) comments on Minoan destruction as being *'...especially directed...towards a class or elite'*. The Maya Book of Chilam Balaam (Joyce and Weller 2007) writes of severe oppression of commoners who expressed resistance through ritual and destruction and defacement of monuments and other symbols of elite rule – but after collapse (Joyce, Bustamente, Levine 2001). Evidence of socially differentiated skeletal trauma, indicating class violence has been found at Harappa sites, but the evidence suggests not violence by the poor against the rich but the reverse.

The most telling archaeological evidence is that of Kohler and Ellyson (2018 p.145.) found that peak violence was contemporaneous with or followed peaks in inequality. A lagged relationship such as this may explain why, unsurprisingly, so many modern regression analyses using contemporaneous data on violence and inequality find little if any correlation (p. 30 above). However the Pueblo skeletal evidence does not appear to have been analysed to establish whether any social differentiation in the trauma is present nor any correlation with political instability (Levitt 2019).

Conclusions

Inequalities accompanied by popular grievance were indisputable features of ancient states discussed above. But for grievance to translate into political revolt leadership and organisation are needed- something the Bacaudae seem to have provided although the details are obscure. They appear to have attracted some members of the alienated peasantry while some of the latter seem to have welcomed and collaborated with the barbarian invaders, if Salvian and Zosimus are to be believed. However the contribution of inequality to alienation, enemy collaboration and revolt to the fall of Rome has not been robustly established.

Although the written evidence of commoner revolt from the Western Roman Empire is disputed it seems plausible, having been provided by eye witnesses, despite scepticism about their motives. But that from the Old Kingdom is highly contentious but reveals concern about commoner alienation and hostility as at least potential threats to stability.

Regarding archaeological evidence, the hypothesis that a revolt by lower class Dorians caused or contributed to Mycenaean collapse is not supported by evidence. Destruction and defacements of symbols of elite Mycenaean structures seems to have expressed commoner resentment, as with the Maya. But such damage is consistent with the possibility that it followed but did not initiate or contribute significantly to the collapse of political authority.

The most significant archaeological evidence of a link between inequality and civil disorder is the skeletal remains from Mesoamerican pueblo societies. However, as with Mycenaean skeletal remains, no analysis of possible socially differentiated trauma has been published (where skeletal height or tooth health could be class markers). Nonetheless it suggests a clear, but, lagged relationship between internal violence and inequality.

In any event, the contribution of inequality to political collapse is complex: violence is not necessarily intended to achieve collapse; violent revolt can be insufficient to provoke collapse if unaccompanied by leadership and organisation; moreover the degree of the effectiveness of state repression and the degree of cohesion among rulers and the governing elite of are crucial.

The Issue of the extent to which inequality contributed to ancient collapse has been neglected in the literature, perhaps because of (i) the paucity of archaeological evidence or failure to bring together such evidence as there is (ii) lack of interest or (iii) dearth of rigorous analysis of possible social differentiation in skeletal trauma, which itself may reflect lack of interest (Levitt 2019).

VIII. Summary and Conclusions

The analysis emphasised the importance of distinguishing between states and civilisations, a matter often sidestepped by those who deny the existence of collapse. It considers the possible origins of states, different theoretical models of state emergence and development, the fragility of ancient states and theories of the cyclicality of state formation and collapse.

No consensus is found for the meaning of collapse. Several different markers of collapse are considered but it is noted that few have investigated evidence of socially differentiated skeletal trauma as an indicator of possible social strife. Several possible explanations of collapse are discussed and found inadequate because, apart from Turchin, they ignore systems dynamics.

Turning to the case studies, although political collapse of the Old Kingdom is definite there is no consensus on the scope and severity of economic and cultural collapse. Drought, famine and intra-elite strife have been suggested as explanations for collapse but the chapter concludes that the evidence is of systems failure and dysfunctionality including the incompetence and collapse of central authority and intra-elite strife (not least centre-provincial conflict); failure to finance and maintain key water management infrastructures; drought, the effects of which were exacerbated by that failure; loss of asibaya induced by huge inequality and the behaviour of selfish elites; and social conflict, possibly violent.

The political collapse of the Mycenaean palace states is beyond dispute. Some but not all aspects of their civilisation vanished. However explanations of their political collapse are particularly speculative because the very existence of some possible explanatory factors is poorly demonstrated in the archaeological and written record.

The WRE was dismantled by successive 'Barbarian' invasions which should be regarded as factors in a dynamic systems collapse: ineffectual, corrupt governments, dynastic rivalry, intra-elite strife, economic and fiscal weakness and reduced military budgets induced barbarian invasion which further reduced the tax base and military funding. Aggressive imperial expansion itself had induced Germanic tribal coalescence which then exploited emerging Roman weakness and dismembered the WRE. The collapse graphically illustrates failure to meet the conditions needed for stability: effective defence against external attack, robust public finances, intra-elite cohesion, a society-wide spirit of asibaya, commoner and elite acceptance of the legitimacy of the ruling regime, including willingness to support the state in the face of external attack.

The collapse of classic Maya states embraced the end of a political system and material culture but at different times in different places. Violent dynastic and intra-elite strife are probably sufficient to explain collapse; but they would have contributed to ineffectual responses to climate change, especially drought. Droughts arose at different times in different locations, although agriculture seems to have continued in some arid areas and evidence of drought in one place cannot explain collapse elsewhere. In short, ineffective government associated with internal strife along with droughts induced collapse but their relative contributions probably varied across the Maya states.

No analysis of inequality as an explanation of ancient collapse has been attempted or even suggested in recent publications on either ancient inequality or collapse. Evidence of inequality exists: house and skeletal size, and grave goods demonstrate ancient inequality. But grievance induced by inequality alone is insufficient to provoke successful challenge to authority; leadership, organisation and resources are also needed. They were conceivably provided by the WRE Bacaudae but their role in WRE collapse is disputed although written evidence suggests discontented peasants sometime welcomed and assisted barbarian invaders. Violence by the poor is suggested as a factor in Old Kingdom and Mycenaean collapse but the evidence is disputed in both cases. Minoan and Mayan evidence of damage to elite property exists but it is not known whether this preceded or followed collapse of authority. One Pueblo study demonstrates correlation between peak inequality and peak violence but no examination of possible socially differentiated skeletal trauma was undertaken. Such research could produce useful evidence of possible social strife as a factor in collapse. Lack of such evidence could indicate lack of interest in inequality's contribution to collapse or its genuine unavailability.

Tables 3 and 4 below summarise the main findings.

The Old Kingdom and Mayan collapses conceivably might fit the mono-causal linear model with internal strife or drought-induced famine being sufficient explanations. However the interaction of drought and failure to take adequate precautions because of strife- ravaged government seems more plausible. The Western Roman Empire illustrates dynamic recursive system interactions: invasions induced by internal strife, economic mismanagement, stressed public finances and consequential military weakness which led to further fiscal inadequacy and irresistible invasion. Mycenaean collapse is susceptible to many explanations, if the need for robust evidence is eschewed, but is an enigma. Elements of dysfunctionality are common to all the case studies.

Table 3. Summary of evidence of collapse

Evidence	Old Kingdom	Mycenae	WRE	Maya
Disappearance/reduced central authority	Y	Y	Y	Y
State fragmentation	Y	NA	Y	Y
Reduced territory		NA	Y	Y
Destruction/abandonment	Y	Y	Y	Y
End/reduced monumental construction	Y	Y	Y	Y
Population fall/dispersal	Y	Y	Y	Y
Reduced economic/agricultural production	?/Y	Y	Y	Y
Decline/ending of art/writing/crafts	?	Y	y/?	Y

Table 4. Explanations for collapse

Cause	Old Kingdom	Mycenae	Rome	Maya
Erosion of legitimacy	Y	?	Y	?
Loss of asibaya	Y	?	Y	Y
Intra-elite strife	Y	Y/?	Y	Y
Excessive/regressive taxation	Y/?	?	Y	?
Inadequate revenues	Y	?	Y	?
Poor maintenance of civil/military infrastructures	Y	?	Y	?
Invasion/inter-state war	N	Y/?	Y	Y
Natural disaster	Y	?	N/?	Y
Human ecological damage	N	N	?	Y/?
Excessive inequality	Y	?	Y	?/Y
Class conflict	Y	Y/?	Y	?/Y
Systems collapse	Y	Y	Y	Y
Costly excessive complexity	Y	?	Y	?

Bibliography

Amiers J., 2011, *Drought and the Maya* Forum, Societal Collapse, Nature Vol. 479, Nov. 3 2011 pp 44-45

Atkins M. and Osborne R., 2006, *Poverty in the Roman World*, Cambridge, Cambridge University Press

Atkinson A.B. 2015, *Inequality*, Harvard, Harvard University Press

Bar-Yosef O. and Meadow R., 1995, *The Origins of Agriculture in the Near East* in Price T. and Gebauer G. (Eds.) 1995, *Last Hunter Gatherers*, New School of American Research Press, Santa Fe

Bard K., 2000, *The Emergence of the Egyptian State* in Shaw N. (Ed.), *The Oxford History of Ancient Egypt*, Oxford, Oxford University Press

Bell B., 1971, *The Dark Ages in Ancient Egypt: The First Dark Age*, American Journal of Archaeology 75 pp 1 – 26

Bell C., 2006, *The Evolution of Long Distance Trading Relationships Across the LBA/Iron Age Transition on the Northern Levantine Coast*, Oxford, BAR International Series 1574 Archaeopress

Bennett J., 1999, *Pylos: the Expansion of a Mycenaean Centre* in Galaty M.L. and Parkinson W.A. (Eds.), *Rethinking Mycenaean Palaces*, 2007, Cotsen Institute of Archaeology, University of California

Betzenhauser A., 2018, *Exploring Measures of Inequality in The Mississippi Heartland* in Kohler and Smith (op. cit.), 2018

Bintliff J 2012 *The Complete Archaeology of Greece,* Chichester, Wiley

Blanton R., 1990, *Review* of *Tainter 1988, Collapse of Complex Societies,* American Anthropology 55 (2) pp 423 - 441

Boardman J., Griffin J. and Murray O. (Eds.) 1986, *Oxford History of the Classical World*, Oxford, Oxford University Press

Bogerhoff (and seven others) 2010 *Pastoralism and Inequality,* Current Anthropology Vol. 51, 1, pp. 35-47

Boix C., 2008, *Economic Routes of Civil War and Revolution in the Contemporary World*, World Politics vol. 60 (3), pp 390 - 437

Boix C., 2015, *Political Order and Inequality: Their Foundations and Consequences for Human Welfare,* Cambridge, Cambridge University Press

Boix C. and Rosenbluth F., 2014, *Bones of Contention: The Political Economy of Height Inequalities*, American Political Science Review 108, pp 1 - 22

Bowersock G., 1996, *The Vanishing Paradigm of the Fall of Rome*, Bulletin of the American Academy of Arts and Sciences 49 No 8, May 1996, pp 29 – 43

Bowersock G., 1991, *Review* of *Tainter, Collapse of Complex Societies*, Journal of Field Archaeology 18 (1), pp 119 – 121

Bronson B., 1988, *The Role of Barbarians in the Fall of States* in Cowgill and Yoffee (op. cit.)

Brown P, 1971 *The World of Late Antiquity* London, Thames and Hudson

Buhag H., Cederman L-K., Gleditch K., 2011, *Square Pegs in Round Holes: Inequalities, Grievances and Civil War*, Paper Presented at Annual Meeting of American Political Science Association Seattle, 1 - 4 September 2011

Butzer K. and Enfield G., 2012, *Critical Perspectives on Collapse*, Proceedings of the National Academy of Science, 109 (10), p 362

Butzer K., 1980, *Civilisations: Organisations or Systems*, American Scientist vol. 68, 5, pp 517 – 523

Cameron A. and Gamsey P. (Eds.) 1997, *Cambridge Ancient History*, Cambridge, Cambridge University Press

Carniero R., 1970, *A Theory of the Origin of the State*, Science 1970, pp 733 – 739

Carpenter R., 1996, *Discontinuity in Greek Civilisation*, Cambridge, Cambridge University Press

Cherry J.F., 1978, *Generalization and the Archaeology of the State* in Green D., Haselgrove C., Spriggs M., *Social Organisation and Settlement*, British Archaeological Reports, International Series Supplementary 47 (ii), pp 411 – 438

Cherry J.F., 1984, *The Emergence of the State in the Prehistoric Aegean*, Proceedings of the Cambridge Philological society, 30, pp. 18-48

Cline E. (Ed.), 2009, *Oxford Handbook of the Bronze Age Aegean*, Oxford, Oxford University Press

Cline E., 2014, *1177 B.C. The Year Civilization Collapsed*, Princeton, Princeton University Press

Collier P. and Hoeffler A., 2004, *Greed and Grievance*, Oxford Economic Papers 56 (4), pp 603 – 695

Cook C., 2013 *Long Run Health Effects of the Neolithic revolution* Working Draft, Yale School of Public Health

Cook J., *Ice Age Art*, British Museum, p.67

Couper G. and Howe G., 2016, *Gallic Insurgencies? Annihilating the Bagaudae* in *Brill's Companion to Insurgency and Terrorism in the Ancient Mediterranean*, pp 312 – 343

Cumming G. and Peterson G., 2018, *Unifying Research on Social – Ecological Resilience and Collapse* in Trends in Ecology and Evolution, Sept. 2017, vol. 32.9

Cunliffe B., 2008, *Europe Between the Oceans: Themes and variations: 9000BC-AD 1000* Yale University Press, New Haven

Dark K., 1998, *Waves of Time: Long Term Change and International Relations*, New York, Continuum

Darnell B, Menassa C 2007, *Tutankhamun's Armies* Wiley, Hoboken NJ

Deger – Jalkotzy S., 2008, *Decline, Destruction, Aftermath* in Schelmerdine (Ed.), *Cambridge Companion to Bronze Age Aegean*, Cambridge, Cambridge University Press

Deger – Jalkotzy S. and Lemos I. (Eds.), 2006, *Ancient Greece from the Mycenaean Palaces to the Age of Homer*, Edinburgh, Edinburgh University Press

Demandt A, 1984, *Der Fall Roms*, Munich, Beck Verlag

Demarest et. al. 1997, *Classic Maya Defensive Systems and Warfare in the Petexbatun Region: Archaeological Evidence and Interpretation*, Ancient Mesoamerica 8, pp 229 – 263

Diamond J., 2005, *Collapse: How Societies Choose to Fail or Survive*, London, Penguin

Diamond J., 2007, *Guns, Germs and Steel*, London, Vintage

Dickinson O., 1974, *Draught and the Decline of Mycenae*, Antiquity 48, pp 228 – 230

Dickinson O., 2006, *The Aegean From the Bronze Age to the Iron Age*, London, Routledge

Dobson A and Carper, E, 1996, *Infectious Diseases and Human Population History*, Bioscience Feb., Vol. 46, 2 pp. pp.115-126

Drake B., 2012, *The Influence of Climactic Change on the Late Bronze Age Collapse and The Greek Dark Ages*, Journal of Archaeological Science 39, pp 1862 – 1870

Driessen J., 1997, *The Troubled Island*, Liege, University of Liege

Drinkwater J., 1992, *The Bacaudae of Fifth Century Gaul* in Drinkwater J. and Elton H. (Eds.), *Fifth Century Gaul: A Crisis of Identity*, Cambridge, Cambridge University Press

Drews R., 1993, *The End of the Bronze Age*, Princeton, Princeton University Press

Duhoux Y. And Davies A, 2008, *Companion to Linear B Vol. 1*, Louvain La Neuve, Peeters

Earle T. (Ed.) 1997, *How Chiefs Come to Power*, Stanford, Stanford University Press

Earle T., 1997, *A Reappraisal of Redistribution: Complex Hawaiian Chiefdoms* in Earle T., Ericson J., *Exchange Systems in Prehistory*, New York, Academic Press

Faulkner R., 1965, *The Admonition of an Egyptian Sage*, Journal of Egyptian Archaeology vol. 51, pp 53 – 65

Feinman G., 2011, *Comparative Frames for the Diachronic Analysis of Complex Societies* in Smith M.E., *Comparative Archaeology of Complex Societies*, Cambridge, Cambridge University Press

Feinman G. and Marcus J., 1998, *Archaic States*, Santa Fe, School of American Research Press, pp 59 – 91,

Finne M., Holmgren K., Chuan – Chou Shen, Hsung – Ming Hu, Boyd M., Stocker S., *Late Bronze Age Climate Change and the Destruction of the Mycenaean Palace of Nestor at Pylos;* Plos One (12) 12 0189447

Fried M., 1960, *On the Evolution of Social Stratification and the State* in Diamond S., *Culture History Essays in Honour of Paul Roden*, New York, Columbia University Press

French E., 2010, *Mycenae* in Cline E., op. cit.

Gagneux S, 2012, *Host-pathogen co evolution in human tuberculosis Philosophical Transactions,* Royal Society of London, Biological Science Vol. 367 (1590 PNC 3267123) pp. 850-859

Galaty M. and Parkinson W. (Eds.) 2009, *Archaic State Interaction: the East Mediterranean in the Bronze Age*, Santa Fe School for Advanced Research

Garcia *War in the Old Kingdom* in Vidal (Ed.) *Studies in the Ancient Near East,* Ugarit Verlag, Munich

Garnsey P., 1998, *Cities, Peasants and Food in Classical Antiquity*, Cambridge, Cambridge University Press

Gibbon E., 1978 (1781), *Decline and Fall of the Roman Empire*, London, Penguin Classics

Goffart W., 1980, *Barbarians and Romans,* Princeton, Princeton University Press

Goldstone J., 1991, *Revolution and Rebellion in the Early Modern World*, Berkeley, University of California Press

Grey C., 2006, *Salvian, the Ideal Christian Community and the Fate of the Poor* in Atkins and Osborne, op. cit.

Groube L., 1996, *The impact of Diseases on the Emergence of Agriculture* in Harris D. (Ed.) *The origins and spread of agriculture and pastoralism in Eurasia* Washington DC, Smithsonian Institute Press

Haas J., 1981, *Class Conflicts and the State in the New World* in Jones G. and Kautz R. (Eds.) *The Transition to Statehood in the New World*, Cambridge, Cambridge University Press, pp 80 – 102

Heather P., 2005, *The Fall of the Roman Empire* , London Macmillan

Halsall G., 2007, *Barbarian Migrations and the Roman West*, Cambridge, Cambridge University Press

Hibbs D., 1973, *Mass Political Violence*, New York, Wiley

Hodder I., 2003, *Reading the Past*, Cambridge, Cambridge University Press

Hutson S., 2016, *The Ancient Urban Maya,* University press of Florida

Ibn Khaldun, 1958 (1337), *The Muqaddina, An Introduction to History*, New York, Pantheon

Ivakovou M., 1999, *The Greek Exodus to Cyprus*, Mediterranean Historical Review 14, 2, pp 1 - 28

Johnson N., 2007, *Simply Complexity: A Clear Guide to Complexity Theory*, Oxford, One World Publications.

Jones A., 1964, *The Later Roman Empire*, University of Oklahoma Press

Jones G. and Kautz R. (Eds.) 1981, *Transition to Statehood in the New World*, Cambridge, Cambridge University Press

Joyce A., Bustamente A. and Levine M., 2001, *Commoner Power, A Case Study for the Classic Period in the Collapse on the Oaxaca*, Journal of Archaeological Method and Theory 8, 4

Joyce A. and Weller E., 2007, *Commoner Ritual, Resistance and the Classic to Postclassic Transition in Ancient Mesoamerica* in Gonlin N. and Lohse J., *Commoner Ritual and Ideology in Ancient Mesoamerica*, pp 143 – 184, Boulder, University of Colorado Press

Judson S 1968, *Erosion Rates Near Rome, Science* 160, 1444-1446

Kaniewski D., Guiot J. and Van Campo E., 6th May 2015, *Environmental Routes of the Late Bronze Age Collapse*, Wiley Online Library, WIRES, Climate Change

Kemp B., 1983, *The Old Kingdom, the Middle Kingdom and the Second Intermediate Period* in Trigger B., Kemp B., O'Connor D. and Lloyd A., *Ancient Egypt, a Social History*, pp 71 – 112, Cambridge University Press

Killen 2004, *Mycenaean Economy* in Duhoux and Davies op. cit.

Kilian K., 1996, *Earthquakes and Archaeological Context* in Stiros S. and Jones R. (Eds.) *Archaeoseismology*, Athens, The British School at Athens and the Institute of Geology and Mineral Exploration, p 63 – 68

Kohler T. and Ellyson L., 2018, *In and Out of Change. The Changing Social Context, the Pueblo South West AD 600 - 1300* in Kohler and Smith op. cit. pp 130 – 145

Kohler T. and Smith M., 2018, *Ten Thousand Years of Inequality. The Archaeology of Wealth Differences*, Tucson, University of Arizona Press

Kromm M. et al, 2002, *Nile River Sediment Fluctuations Over the Past 7000 Years and their Key Role*, Geology 30 (1), pp 71 – 74

Lancon B., 2000, *Rome in Late Antiquity*, Edinburgh, Edinburgh University Press

Lee A., 1997, *The Army* in Cameron and Gamsey op. cit.

Legarra Herrero B., 2014, *Mortuary Behaviour and Social trajectories in Pre-Palatial Crete,* London, UCL, ProQuest Dissertation Publishing U 232716

Legarrara Herrero B., 2016, *Primary State Formation Processes in Crete*, Cambridge Archaeological Journal, Jul. 2016 26:2

Levitt M., 2019, *The neglected Role of Inequality,* Cliodynamics, 10:1, 2019
Lichbach M., 1989, *An Evaluation of 'Does Economic Inequality Breed Political Conflict?',* World Politics 41, pp 431 – 470
Little K (Ed.) 2006, *Plague and the End of Antiquity,* Cambridge, CUP
MacCulloch R., 2005, *Income Inequality, the Taste for Revolution,* Journal of Law and Economics, Vol. 48 1, pp 93 – 123
MacMullan R., 1990, *Corruption and the Decline of Rome,* Yale, Yale University Press
Malek J., 2000, *The Old Kingdom* in Shaw op. cit.
Mann M., 1986, The Sources of Social Power Vol. 1, Cambridge, CUP
Manning J., 2013, *The Oxford Handbook of the State in the Ancient Near East and the Mediterranean,* Oxford, Oxford University Press
Maran J., 2009, *The Crisis Years? Reflections on Signs of Instability in the Last Decades of the Mycenaean Palaces,* Rome, Universita Degli Studi Di Roma 'La Sapienza'
Maran J., 2010, *Tiryns* in Cline op. cit.
Marius J., 1998, *The Peaks and Valleys of Ancient States and Civilisations* in Feinman and Marcus op. cit.
McAnany P. and Yoffee N., 2010, *Questioning Collapse,* Cambridge, Cambridge University Press
McGuire R., 1983, *Breakdown in Cultural Complexity,* Journal in Advances in Archaeological Method and Theory vol. 6, pp 91 – 142
Middleton G., 2010, *The Collapse of Palatial Society in Late Bronze Age Greece and the Postpalatial Period,* Oxford, BAR International Series 2110
Middleton G., 2017, *Understanding Collapse,* Cambridge, Cambridge University Press
Moeller N., 2005, *The First Intermediate Period: a Time of Famine and Climate Change?* Egypt and the Levant, 1 January 2005, Vol. 15 pp 153 – 167
Moholy-Nagy H., 1994, *Tikal Material Culture: Artefacts and social structure at classic lowland Maya City,* University of Michigan, ProQuest Dissertation publishing 9423270
Moholy-Nagy H., 2016, *Set in Stone: Hiatuses and Dynastic Politics at Tikal,* Ancient Mesoamerica, 27, pp. 255-266, CUP.
Moorhead J., 2001, *The Roman Empire Divided 400-700,* London, Pearson
Muller E., 1985, *Income Inequality, Regime Repression and Political Violence,* American Social Science Review 50, 1, Feb. 1985, pp 47 – 61
Muller J., Arponen J., Hofman R. And Ohlrav R., 2015, *Appearance of Social Inequalities: Cases of Neolithic and Chalcolith Sites,* Origini XXXVIII, 2015, 2, Sapienza, University of Rome
Nur A. and Cline E., 2000, *Poseidon's Horses: Plate Tectonics and Earthquake Storms in the Late Bronze Age Aegean and Eastern Mediterranean,* Journal of Archaeological Science 27, pp 43 – 63
Ortmans O., Mazzeo E., Mescherina K., 2017, *Modelling Social Pressure Towards Instability in the United Kingdom after 1960: A Demographic Structural Analysis,* Cliodynamics, 8 (2)
Parker Pearson M., 1982, *Mortuary Practice, Societies and Ideology* in Hodder I. (Ed.) *Symbolic and Structural Archaeology,* Cambridge, Cambridge University Press
Parkinson R., 1997, *The Tale of Sinue and Other Ancient Egyptian Poems,* Oxford, Oxford University Press
Pohl W., 2005, *Justinian and the Barbarian Kingdoms* in Maas M., *The Cambridge Companion to the Age of Justinian,* Cambridge, Cambridge University Press, pp 448 – 474
Potter D., 2009, *Rome in the Ancient World: From Romulus to Justinian,* London, Thames and Hudson
Prentiss M., Foor T. and Murphy M., 2018, *Testing Hypothesise about Emerging Inequality Using Gini Coefficients in a Complex Fisher - Foraging Society at the Bridge River Sit, British Columbia* in Kohler and Smith op. cit. pp 96 – 129
Quirko H., 2005, *Review, How Societies Choose to Fail or Succeed,* American Anthropologist 1 December 2005, Vol. 107 (4), pp 724
Redman C., 2005, *Resilience Theory in Archaeology,* American Anthropologist 107 (1), pp 70 – 77
Renfrew C., 1972, *The Emergence of Civilisation,* London, Methuen

Renfrew C., 1979, *Systems Collapse as Social Transformation* in Renfrew C. and Cooke C., *Transformations, Mathematical Approaches to Culture*, New York, The Academic Press

Robbins Schug G., Gray K., Mushrif – Tripathy V., Sankhyan A., 2012, *A Peaceful Realm? Trauma and Social Differentiation at Harrapa*, International Journal of Paleopathology, Vol. 2 (2-3), pp 136 – 147

Robinson J., 1904, *Readings in European History*, Boston, Fordham Medieval Source Book, pp 28 – 30

Rutter J., 1992, *Cultural Novelties in the Post-Palatial Aegean World* in Ward and Joukowsky op. cit.

Sandars N., 1978, *The Sea Peoples: Warriors of the Ancient Mediterranean*, London, Thames and Hudson Publishers

Scott J., 2017, *Against the Grain: A Deep History of the Earliest States*, Yale, Yale University Press

Shaw I. (Ed.) 2000, *The Oxford History of Ancient Egypt*, Oxford, Oxford University Press

Scheidel W., 2006, *Stratification, Deprivation and Quality of Life* in Atkins and Osborne op. cit.

Scheidel W., 2017, *The Great Leveler: Violence and the History of Inequality from the Stone Age to the Twenty - First Century*, Princeton, Princeton University Press

Shennan S., 2011, *Property and Inequality as Cultural Niche* Philosophical Transactions of the Royal Society 366, 921

Shennan S., 2018, *The First Farmers of Europe, An Evolutionary Perspective,* Cambridge World Archaeology, Cambridge

Schepartz L., Miller – Antonio S., Murphy J., 2010, *Differential Health and the Mycenaean Messen Status, Sex and Dental Health at Pylos* in Schepartz L., Fox S., Bourbou C. (Eds.) *New Directions in the Skeletal Biology of Greece*, Princeton, Princeton University Press, pp 155 – 174

Schwartz G., 2006, *From Collapse to Regeneration* in Schwartz G. and Nichols G. (Eds.) *After Collapse: the Regeneration of Complex Societies*, Tucson, University of Arizona Press

Seidelmayer S., 2000, *The First Intermediate Period* in Shaw, 2000, op. cit.

Service E.R., 1962, *Primitive Social Organization, an Evolutionary Perspective,* Random House, New York

Storey R . And Storey G, 2017, *Rome and the Classic Maya,* London, Routledge

Tainter J., 1988, *The Collapse of Complex Societies*, Cambridge, Cambridge University Press

Tainter J., 2004, *Plotting the Downfall of Society* in Nature vol. 427 (6974), Feb. 2004, pp 488 – 489

Tainter J., 2006, *Archaeology of Overshoot and Collapse*, Annual Review of Anthropology 35, pp 59 – 74

Tainter J. and Crumley C., 2007, *Climate, Complexity and Problem Solving in the Roman Empire* in Constanza R., Gramlich L. And Steffen W. *Sustainability and Collapse,* Cambridge Mass., MIT Press

Thompson E., 1952, *Peasant Revolts in Late Roman Gaul and Spain*, Past and Present No 2, Nov. 1952, pp 11 – 23

Tocqueville A., De, (1835) 1961, *Democracy in America*, New York, Schocken Books

Trinkhaus et. al., *The people of Sunghir: burials, bodies and behaviour in nthe early upper Palaeolithic*, Oxford University Press

Turchin P., 2003, *Historical Dynamics: Why States Rise and Fall*, Princeton, Princeton University Press

Turchin P. and Korotayev A., 2006, *Population Dynamics and Internal Warfare: a Reconsideration*, Social Evolution and History vol. 5, No 2, Sep. 2006, pp 112 – 147

Turchin P. and Nefedov S., 2009, *Secular Cycles*, Princeton, Princeton University Press

Turchin P., 2016, *Ages of Discord* Beresta Books, Chaplin, Conn.

Van De Mieroop M, 2010, *The Eastern Mediterranean in the Age of Ramases II*, Chichester, Wiley

Van De Mieroop M., 2011, *A History of Ancient Egypt*, Oxford, Blackwell

Voutsakis S., Trantaphyllou S., Ingvarsson – Sundstron A., Sarri K., Richards M., Nijboer A., Kouidou – Andreou S., Kovatsi L., Nikou D. and Milka E., 2006, *Project On the Middle Helladic Argolid: A Report on the 2006 Season*; Athens, Pharos: Journal of the Netherlands Institute in Athens vol. XIV (2006)

Wagner M. and 20 others, Yersina *Pestis and the Plague of Justinian,* Lancet, 2014 Infectious Diseases Vol. 14, no. 4, pp. 319-326

Wallbank F., 1969, *The Awful Revolution: the Decline of the Roman Empire in the West*, Toronto, Toronto University Press

Ward – Perkins B., 2005, *The Fall of Rome and the End of Civilisation*, Oxford, Oxford University Press
Ward W. and Joukowsky M. (Eds.) 1992, *The Crisis Years: the 12th Century B.C. From Beyond the Danube to the Tigris*, Dubuqe Iowa, Kendall/Hunt
Webster D., 2002, *The Fall of the Ancient Maya*, London, Thames and Hudson
Whitby M., 1997, *The Army 420 – 602* in Cameron and Gamsey op. cit.
Wilkinson T., 2010, *The Rise and Fall of Ancient Egypt*, London, Bloomsbury
Wilkinson O., , *The Formation of Mycenaean Palaces* in Deger – Jalkotzy, 2008, op. cit.
Yoffee N. and Cowgill G. (Eds.) 1988, *The Collapse of Ancient States and Civilisations*, Tucson, Arizona University Press
Yoffee N., 2005, *Myths of the Ancient State*, Cambridge, Cambridge University Press
Zeder M., 2011, *The Origins of Agriculture in the Near East*, Current Anthropology 52 No S4: pp 221 – 235